616.97 SIL

Silverstein, Alvin.

AIDS : deadly threat

616.97 SIL

Silverstein, Alvin.

AIDS : deadly threat

AUG 28 '87
MAR 2
MAR 29
APR 12

DATE DUE

AUG 28 '87
MAR 2
MAR 29
APR 12

BORROWER'S NAME

AIDS:
DEADLY THREAT

ALVIN and VIRGINIA SILVERSTEIN

ENSLOW PUBLISHERS, INC.

Bloy St. & Ramsey Ave.   P.O. Box 38
Box 777   Aldershot
Hillside, N.J. 07205   Hants GU12 6BP
U.S.A.   U.K.

ACKNOWLEDGMENTS

The authors are deeply grateful to Dr. James Curran of the Centers for Disease Control, Richard Dunne of the Gay Men's Health Crisis, and Dr. Paul Volberding of San Francisco General Hospital, who found time in their busy schedules for a careful reading of the manuscript. Their many helpful comments and suggestions and the insight and perspective that they provided were invaluable. Thanks, too, to our editor, Patricia Culleton, for her encouragement and help at all stages of the project.

Library of Congress Cataloging-in-Publication Data

Silverstein, Alvin.
   AIDS : deadly threat.

   Includes bibliography and index.
   1. AIDS (Disease)–Popular works. I. Silverstein,
Virginia B. II. Title. [DNLM: 1. Acquired
Immunodeficiency Syndrome–popular works.
WD 308 S587a]
RC607.A26S56   1986   616.97'92   85-23393
ISBN 0-89490-128-1

Printed in the United States of America

10 9 8 7 6 5 4 3 2

Illustration Credits
Centers for Disease Control, pp. 20, 41, 80, 89; Wide World
Photos, Inc., pp. 49, 63, 69, 73.

Contents

Foreword

Since 1981, an epidemic of acquired immune deficiency syndrome—AIDS—has caused the death of thousands in the United States and untold thousands in other parts of the world. Fear of the disease has been rampant, largely due to a lack of understanding about the nature of the AIDS virus. Scientists know a great deal about the virus; they understand that by taking the proper precautions, AIDS can be prevented. It is vital for everyone to know the facts about the disease. Education is our most effective weapon against its spread.

AIDS: Deadly Threat is directed mainly to young people and explains, in accurate and straightforward terms, much of what is currently understood about AIDS. The authors have done an excellent job of making a complex disease understandable. This book points out that AIDS is not a mysterious killer—it can be stopped.

It is particularly important that the facts about this disease reach young people at a time when they are considering future lifestyles and sexual practices. *AIDS: Deadly Threat* fills an important role in education. This book should be required reading for young people of all ages.

Paul Volberding, M.D.

Chief, Medical Oncology and
    Director, AIDS Activities
    San Francisco General Hospital.

Assistant Professor of Medicine
    Cancer Research Institute
    University of California, San Francisco

1

Deadly Threat

If you read the daily newspaper or watch the news on TV, you may get the impression that our number-one health problem today is a disease called AIDS. And yet, the number of victims is only a fraction of the toll claimed annually by such major killers as heart disease and cancer. Each year three quarters of a million Americans die of heart disease and close to half a million die of cancer. Compared with numbers like those, the few thousand who die of AIDS every year seem almost insignificant. Why, then, is everybody so frightened?

First of all, AIDS is a new disease. Cancer and heart disease have been killing people as long as there have been humans on the earth. But scientists didn't even find out about AIDS until 1981. Second, although the numbers are still small, the reported total of AIDS cases in the United States is currently doubling each year. A third frightening factor is the deadliness of the new disease. Most AIDS victims die within two years.

When AIDS first appeared in America, it seemed to be confined to only a few small groups of the population, concentrated in a few large cities. Now the danger is spreading.

AIDS is appearing in an ever-growing number of cities and towns throughout the United States and in other countries all over the world—and it is striking people from groups that were believed to be "safe."

The AIDS epidemic is giving rise to another growing epidemic: fear. In some cities, parents are fearful that their children may catch AIDS from classmates, and some have even boycotted the schools, keeping their children home. People are abandoning friends and loved ones suffering from the disease for fear that they may get it themselves.

Much of the fear of AIDS comes from ignorance. People don't understand exactly what the disease is and how it is transmitted. Just a few years ago, almost nothing was known about AIDS. Although many mysteries still remain, researchers have come a long way. They have found the cause of the disease and have learned much about the ways it is passed from one person to another. Some of what they have learned is frightening; some is reassuring. There are things that people can do to cut down their chances of getting AIDS. Medical researchers are working on vaccines to prevent the disease and on drugs to cure it.

In the following chapters we will discuss what AIDS is, who is at risk, and the war against it on the medical, social, and political fronts.

2

The Body's Defenses

When the first cases of AIDS began to appear in the United States, it took some time for doctors to realize that a single new disease was involved. Some patients were seriously ill with a very rare type of pneumonia. Others were stricken with an even rarer kind of cancer. Still others suffered from fungus growths, which caked the mouth and throat and made it painful to eat and speak; or from diarrhea caused by microbes, or germs, that are more commonly found in animals. Some patients, less seriously ill, complained of persistent fever, swollen glands in the neck or armpits, and a general feeling of tiredness. What the patients with all these varied ailments had in common was a general breakdown of the body's defenses. Something was interfering with the processes that normally protect people from invading germs or from the growth of cancerous tumors. In the next chapter we'll trace the story of how medical researchers put together the pieces of the AIDS puzzle and isolated the cause of the disease. But first let's describe the body's defenses and the kinds of invaders they are equipped to fight.

A multitude of microbes, each too small to see, swarms in the air we breathe, the food we eat, and every object we touch. Unseen hordes live on the skin of our hands and even in the moist, warm crannies of our mouths. Some of these microbes are harmless; others can cause diseases if they penetrate into the body. The first line of defense against harmful germs is our outer covering, the skin. The various openings into the body may provide entryways for microbes, but they, too, have their defenses. Dust particles, soot, and microbes in the air we inhale are trapped in a layer of gooey mucus and swept out by the action of tiny waving hairlike structures on the cells that line the breathing passages. Natural germ-killing chemicals in tears and saliva help to wipe out the microbes that enter the eyes and mouth, and the acid bath that food receives when it reaches the stomach acts as another effective germ killer. But these defenses aren't perfect, and open cuts or other breaks in the skin or membranes can let microbes slip in.

When microscopic "foreign invaders" penetrate into the body, a number of defenses are called into action. The fever and swelling that often accompany an infection can be uncomfortable and may seem to be hurting the body. Actually they are part of the natural defenses, making it harder for invading germs to survive. When invading microbes damage body tissues, special chemicals are released. These chemicals travel through the blood and act as signals, triggering a series of reactions. Chemicals released by damaged tissues also cause the blood vessels to leak. Watery fluid oozes out into the tissues, producing the swelling of inflammation. This extra fluid in the tissues makes it easier for the body's roving disease fighters, white blood cells, to get around, and they respond quickly to the chemical distress signals.

White blood cells are like tiny animated blobs, that can change their shape, bulging out in one direction or drawing

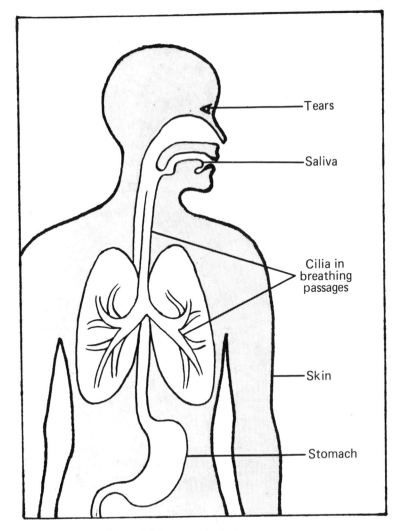

The body's first lines of defense against disease germs.

inward in another. Unlike the other body cells, they move about independently, swimming through the blood or lymph, creeping along the tissues, and moving in and out of blood and lymph vessels with ease by squeezing through tiny gaps between cells. When microbes attack, the first white cells on the scene respond to the threat by eating the invaders. Their jellylike bodies flow over the microbes until the germs are completely enclosed inside the white cells. Then the white cells produce powerful enzymes that break down the microbes, digesting them just as food is digested in the stomach and intestines. One type of white cell that attacks and kills microbes in this way is called the macrophage, which literally means "big eater." As the white cells gobble up microbes, poisons released by the germs build up in the cells. Eventually these poisons kill the white cells. The pus that forms in an infection is made up of the bodies of these dead white-cell defenders and the remains of the microbes they have killed.

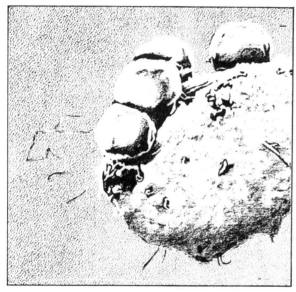

A macrophage in the process of consuming a virus.

Two main kinds of microbes can invade the body and cause disease: bacteria and viruses.

Bacteria are tiny living cells. Each one contains all the necessary working parts of a cell, including a chromosome with chemically coded blueprints for producing all the chemicals the cell needs—and for producing new bacteria. An individual bacterium is too small to be seen without a good microscope. Some bacteria are shaped like little round balls, others like tiny rods, and still others like corkscrews. Each one is enclosed in a tough, protective cell wall made of complicated proteins and carbohydrates. Some bacteria can live peacefully in the body, feeding on the waste products of the food we eat and doing no harm. In fact, some even pay for their keep by producing vitamins the body can use. Others—disease bacteria—produce toxins, poisons that can damage or destroy body tissues.

Each bacterium reproduces by duplicating its genetic material—the chromosome—and then dividing in half. Each half is a tiny, perfect copy of the parent bacterium. It can grow and divide in turn. In the body a bacterium can go through a whole generation in about twenty minutes. That means that without the body's defenses, a single invading bacterium could produce a population numbering in the millions in seven hours—less time than an average night's sleep.

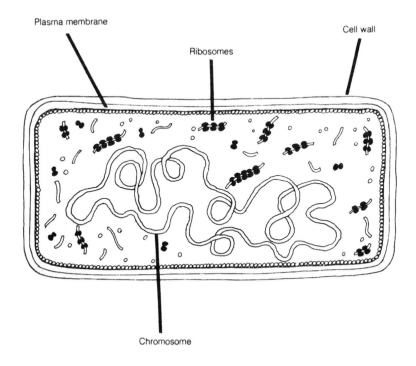

Schematic view of a typical bacterial cell.

Compared to a bacterium, a virus is the ultimate stripped-down, streamlined version of life. Viruses are so simple that many scientists do not consider them really alive. A virus is made up of an inner core of nucleic acid—the genetic material that contains all the hereditary bluebrints—wrapped in a coat made of protein. A virus can't live on its own, and it can't reproduce by itself. It seems to be just a bit of chemical matter until it finds a suitable body cell. Then it goes into action, first attaching itself to the outside of the cell and then slipping inside. There the virus takes over, tricking the cell into making virus chemicals instead of its own. Soon the cell has been turned into a virus-producing factory, making virus cores and coats and putting them together to form new virus particles.

Some viruses live quietly inside a cell. The virus nucleic acid attaches itself to the cell's chromosome and doesn't seem to have much effect. Other viruses run wild, turning all the cell's materials and energy into producing new virus particles. Eventually the cell bursts and dies, spilling out a crop of viruses that can infect other body cells.

Infection of a cell by a virus can trigger another of the body's defenses: the cell is stimulated to produce a protein called interferon. Interferon doesn't help the cell that produced it, but it enters the bloodstream and is carried to other cells. It stimulates those cells to make special antiviral chemicals that protect them from invading viruses. A virus that penetrates into such a protected cell will not be able to turn the cell into a virus factory, and it will not be able to multiply and spread.

Fever, inflammation, the action of macrophages and other germ-eating white blood cells, and interferon—these are all general defenses against invading microbes. The body can also call on some very specialized defenses, each of which works against a particular kind of germ. These defenses are the body's immune system, and the defenders are a type of white blood cells called lymphocytes.

Large numbers of lymphocytes are found in the lymph nodes—which are spongelike masses of tissue in the neck, the armpits, and various other parts of the body. Watery lymph, the fluid that drains out of the tissues and into the bloodstream, flows through channels in the lymph nodes. The nodes act as screening stations, and when the body is invaded by microbes they may become swollen and painful as fierce battles rage inside them. The swollen glands that can be felt during an infection are actually lymph nodes. Lymphocytes are also found in the tonsils and spleen, and they roam through the body, patrolling the tissues in search of foreign invaders.

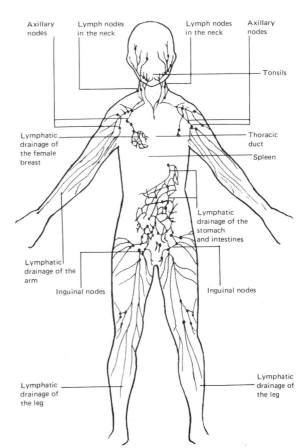

The lymphatic system drains fluid from the body tissues; its lymph nodes are the home for disease-fighting lymphocytes.

There are two main groups of lymphocytes: B cells and T cells. The B cells come from the bone marrow. Their job is to produce proteins called antibodies. Antibody proteins have a sort of Y shape, but the fine details of the structure of different antibodies can vary greatly. In fact, antibodies are so varied that no matter what kind of bacterium, virus, or foreign substance gets into the body, there is likely to be a B cell whose antibodies exactly match some chemical on the invader's surface. These surface chemicals are called antigens, and when an antigen meets the right kind of antibody, it fits into it like a key in a lock. Chemical reactions bind the antigen and antibody together tightly.

When the antigen is on the surface of a bacterium, the antigen-antibody complex acts as a trigger, sparking a series of chemical reactions in the blood that may kill the bacterium or may make it easier for macrophages to mop it up. When antibodies combine with virus antigens, they prevent the viruses from invading body cells. Antibodies can also combine with foreign chemicals, such as bacterial toxins. When that happens, the antibody-antigen complexes link together into long chains, which are then gobbled up by white cells. In each case, once a foreign antigen has been identified, the B cells that produce the right kind of antibodies to destroy it start to multiply. Eventually they may produce enough antibodies to wipe out the invading microbes. Afterward, when the danger is over, larger numbers of those particular B cells are "kept on file" in the body, so that if the same kind of germ invades again, the B cells will be able to respond to the threat more quickly, before a serious infection can get started. The person now has an immunity to the disease that those germs cause and will not become ill the next time they get into the body.

The B cells work closely with the other main group of lymphocytes, the T cells. These lymphocytes get their name from the thymus gland, where they are specially activated for their own jobs. T cells recognize the differences between "self" (the body's own cells and chemicals) and "non-self" (foreign cells and chemicals). Some T cells, called helper T cells, stimulate B cells to multiply and produce antibodies. Other T cells, the suppressor T cells, prevent the B cells from attacking the body's cells. Still other T cells, called killer T cells, can kill foreign invaders by combining with antigens and releasing a powerful battery of chemicals. Killer T cells go to meet the invaders, while B cells normally multiply in the lymph nodes and send their antibodies through the bloodstream. T cells are

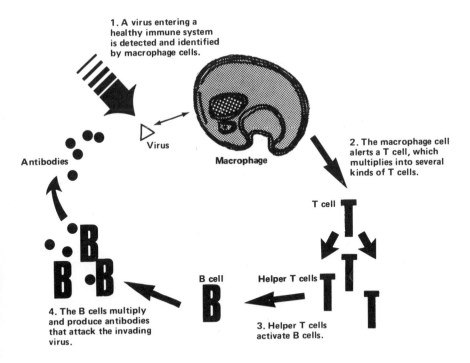

1. A virus entering a healthy immune system is detected and identified by macrophage cells.

Antibodies

Virus

Macrophage

2. The macrophage cell alerts a T cell, which multiplies into several kinds of T cells.

T cell

Helper T cells

B cell

4. The B cells multiply and produce antibodies that attack the invading virus.

3. Helper T cells activate B cells.

The immune system: macrophages, T cells, and B cells cooperate to defend the body against invading microbes.

an important defense against viruses and fungi. They also conduct what scientists call immune surveillance, search-and-destroy missions in which they seek out body cells that have been changed, perhaps by chemicals or radiation or a virus infection, and might multiply into a cancerous tumor.

Important as the T cells are in keeping the body healthy, there are situations in which they can be destructive. When an organ is transplanted from one person to another, there is a danger that it will be rejected—that is, that the body will attack the new organ, killing its cells. Such an attack is led by T cells that have recognized the cells in the transplanted organ as foreign. Doctors try to get around the rejection problem in two ways: by trying to match the person who is donating the organ and the one who is receiving it very carefully, so that their cells are as similar as possible; and by using drugs to suppress the body's immune system, knocking out the T cells that might attack the new organ.

Unfortunately, drugs that suppress the immune system leave a person vulnerable to infections. Microbes that a normal body could easily fight off become life-threatening. Transplant patients also are at more than the usual risk of developing cancer. The problems of transplant patients provided one of the key clues for researchers studying AIDS—. The unusual infections and cancers that AIDS patients were coming down with were ailments that had previously been seen mainly in transplant patients. Something was damaging an AIDS patient's immune system in much the same way as the immunosuppressive drugs that prevent rejection of transplanted organs. The search for that "something" turned into a dramatic medical detective story.

3

Detective Story

"We have never made such rapid progress with any disease in the past." That was what Margaret Heckler, Secretary of Health and Human Services, said in 1984 when scientists announced that the virus causing AIDS had been identified. It was an impressive achievement, but some people say our progress against this deadly new disease hasn't been fast enough. They claim that AIDS has been given a frightening head start, not because of a lack of scientific know-how and skill but because of public attitudes and prejudices. Not enough was done at first, they say, because the first victims of the disease belonged to several specific risk groups, and the general public just didn't feel concerned.

The first few scattered cases of AIDS in the United States appeared in the late 1970s. Nobody realized their significance at the time. They didn't seem to be a single disease. Doctors diagnosed pneumonia, or cancer, or fungus infection, or just some sort of general "bug that's going around," depending on their patients' symptoms. There were so few cases—only eight in the whole country in the years before 1979, eleven in 1979, and forty-six in 1980—that no general pattern was evident.

That situation changed in the winter of 1980–1981. Dr. Michael Gottlieb, an immunologist at UCLA, noticed that in just three months he had treated four patients with a very unusual lung infection. It was a particularly serious kind of pneumonia, often fatal, and it was not caused by the usual pneumonia bacteria or viruses. Matter from the patients' lungs showed the presence of a microorganism called *Pneumocystis carinii.* This is a curious creature. Usually classed as a protozoa (like the amoeba that causes dysentery), it also is somewhat similar to the rare fungi that cause severe illnesses in humans.

Pneumocystis carinii pneumonia (PCP) is normally rare. It is what doctors call an "opportunistic infection," one that develops only in people whose immune systems are already severely weakened, leaving them defenseless against invading microbes. Typically, PCP occurs in someone taking immunosuppressive drugs to prevent rejection of a transplanted organ, or in a patient in the last stages of cancer, when the body's defenses are breaking down. Yet Gottlieb's four PCP patients were all relatively young men, about thirty, who had been fairly healthy until a few months before they developed pneumonia. Questioning the patients about their past health problems and personal backgrounds, Gottlieb could find only one thing in common—they were all gay, and three of the four had had many sex partners.

It was a curious coincidence, and Gottlieb decided it was worth reporting to the national Centers for Disease Control (CDC) in Atlanta. The CDC acts as a general screening center and medical detective bureau, keeping a figurative finger on the nation's pulse by charting the spread of diseases and helping to coordinate medical research efforts. The curious cluster of PCP cases in young men in Los Angeles was reported in an issue of the CDC's publication *Morbidity and Mortality Weekly Report* in June of 1981. CDC researchers

Dr. James Curran and Dr. Harold Jaffee noticed the item and wondered what it might mean. Could some strange new epidemic be starting?

Within a few days, more reports began to come in. Doctors in California and in New York City said that they, too, had noticed cases of opportunistic infections in young homosexual men as far back as 1979. There were cases of pneumocystis pneumonia and also cases of a rare kind of cancer called Kaposi's sarcoma (KS) after its discoverer, Moritz Kaposi. Victims of Kaposi's sarcoma have purplish spots on their skin that look like birthmarks or bruises but are not painful. KS cases seen in the United States before the late 1970s were rather mild, slow-growing cancers, found mainly in elderly men or in transplant patients whose immune defenses were suppressed. This cancer spreads so slowly that eight to thirteen years may pass before it does any serious harm. The patient usually dies of something else.

Another form of KS, found in equatorial Africa, is much more serious. It occurs in children and adolescents and attacks organs and glands, killing within months. This more serious form was the kind of KS that had suddenly begun to appear in a few cities in the United States. Doctors were puzzled and alarmed. As a New York University physician remarked, "One patient was an interesting event; two was an epidemic." A kind of cancer that normally occurred in fewer than one out of one hundred thousand people was suddenly popping up all over.

The CDC formed a special task force to investigate the outbreak previously rare diseases. By mid-1981 they had 116 cases to study. Some had Kaposi's sarcoma, some had pneumocystis pneumonia, and about 10 percent had both. Another 10 percent suffered from a variety of strange infections, including fungus growths in the mouth and throat that made speaking and eating difficult and painful; herpes infections with ulcerlike sores on the mouth or genitals that didn't heal for months; fungus and protozoan infections that are usually found only in animals; and a serious bacterial infection that cave explorers sometimes catch from bats. What these varied infections had in common was that they were all opportunistic, rarely occurring except in people whose immune defenses were damaged.

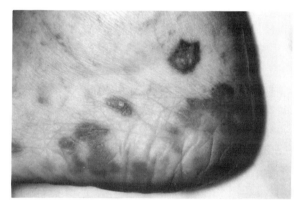

Characteristic purplish spots on the heel and side of the foot of a patient with Kaposi's sarcoma.

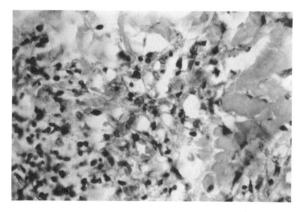

A highly magnified microscopic view of skin tissues in Kaposi's sarcoma.

All of the victims were gay men, about half from New York City and most of the rest from California. They had typically been sexually promiscuous, averaging more than a thousand sex partners each. Such active sex lives had brought a number of medical problems: Most of the men reported that they had suffered at various times from venereal diseases such as syphilis, gonorrhea, and herpes; from hepatitis infections; and from diarrhea-causing parasitic infections. They had been treated with antibiotics for these ailments. They were also heavy users of recreational drugs—particularly forms of nitrites called poppers, which are inhaled to increase the pleasurable feelings of sexual activity.

Medical researchers, speculating on the causes of the new "gay plague," produced a flood of theories. Something these men were doing or coming in contact with was damaging their immune systems. One popular theory speculated about a sort of "immune overload." After so many bouts of sexually transmitted diseases, it was argued, the person's immune defenses were worn-out and couldn't cope any longer. Other researchers thought the poppers were to blame, and some animal experiments indicated that nitrite drugs can damage the immune system.

Another popular theory held that the homosexual sex practices were to blame. Both oral and anal sex could introduce sperm into the body, either by swallowing semen or by its penetration into the bloodstream through tiny tears in the delicate lining of the rectum that often occur during anal sex. Like the cells of an organ transplant, semen contains chemicals that would be recognized as foreign if introduced into another person's body and would thus provoke an immune reaction. There were also animal experiments indicating that sperm in the bloodstream can suppress the immune system. In fact, in experiments with rabbits in which semen was introduced into the rectum artificially, immune suppression was observed even when the rectal lining was undamaged.

These theories sounded plausible, but many medical experts thought that they did not explain the cause of the new disease. They might be contributing factors, but if they were the main cause, why did the disease affect such a small number of gays, concentrated in a few cities? And why did it suddenly appear now and not thousands of years ago?

CDC researchers painstakingly interviewed patients—or relatives, friends, and lovers if the patients had died—and gradually discovered clusters of cases. There was a group of AIDS patients in Los Angeles who had had some sex partners in common. An AIDS patient in New York was found to have been a sexual partner of four of the men in the Los Angeles cluster, as well as four more New York AIDS patients.

The CDC researchers had years of experience in observing how diseases spread, and they recognized a pattern. This was an infectious disease, they said; some kind of microorganism was spreading it, probably a virus. Samples from the AIDS patients—blood, feces, discharges from the breathing passages, bits of tissue—were examined and tested for microorganisms.

Two strong candidates for the AIDS microbe were cytomegalovirus (CMV), a virus that causes mental and physical retardation when children are infected before birth, and Epstein-Barr virus, which causes infectious mononucleosis. Antibodies to both these viruses are found in large percentages of AIDS patients—80 to 95 percent, compared with 50 percent in the general population—and they are present in levels as much as ten to one hundred times the usual value. But when doctors find a virus in a patient with a particular disease, it is very hard to determine whether the virus actually *caused* the disease or is just a tagalong infection. It is even more difficult in the case of AIDS, which attacks the immune defenses and leaves people wide open for a variety of opportunistic infections.

Theories were still being debated when startling new findings changed the picture. As the months went by, new cases of the puzzling disease continued to appear among gay men, and researchers were referring to it as GRID: gay-related immune deficiency. Then the same kinds of illnesses—*Pneumocystis carinii* pneumonia, Kaposi's sarcoma, and various exotic fungus and protozoan infections—began to appear in other groups of the population, too. First they were found in intravenous drug abusers; some of them were gay, but many were not, and some were women. In fact, later studies revealed AIDS virus antibodies in blood taken in 1976 from a female IV drug abuser; this was the earliest documented appearance of the virus in the United States. Other groups soon joined the rolls of the victims: hemophiliacs, who used clotting factors made from blood products to treat their hereditary "bleeders' disease," and recent immigrants from Haiti. Apparently the new epidemic was not an exclusively "gay plague" after all.

The term GRID gave way to AIDS (acquired immune deficiency syndrome), and the theories relating its causes to homosexual sex practices began to fall out of favor. Only a microorganism transmitted either by sexual activity or in blood and blood products could explain the occurrence of AIDS in the new risk groups as well. Since the blood factors taken by hemophiliacs are filtered to remove bacteria and fungi, and they can still transmit AIDS, it seemed that the microorganism responsible for this disease must be a virus. The hunt for the AIDS virus was on.

Scientists are still heatedly debating who really discovered the AIDS virus. Two research teams, one in the United States and the other in France, have good claims. In fact, each team has its own name for the virus, with a list of reasons why its name is better. The debate seems destined to continue for far longer than the amazingly brief time it took to isolate and identify the virus. The prizes for the winners will be great indeed: not only fame and glory—and perhaps a Nobel Prize—for making an important medical discovery, but also money for their research institute from patent rights for tests, vaccines, and treatments based on the discovery. For example, diagnostic kits for screening blood for AIDS antibodies are already a multimilliondollar business.

The American team is headed by Dr. Robert Gallo, Director of the Laboratory of Tumor Cell Biology at the National Cancer Institute in Bethesda, Maryland. In 1980, Gallo discovered the first human cancer virus. He named it HTLV-I, or human T cell leukemia virus, Type I. This virus homes in on T cells, causing them to multiply uncontrollably. HTLV-I is what scientists call a retrovirus. *Retro-* means "backwards," and retroviruses reverse the usual process by which cells translate their hereditary blueprints into the biochemicals they need.

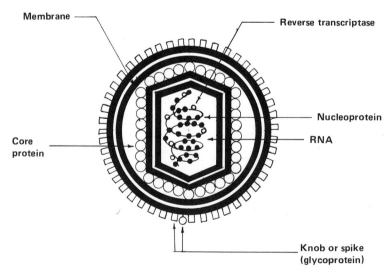

Schematic view of a retrovirus.

Normally a cell's hereditary information is coded in the form of DNA, which is constructed chemically from two long chains of building blocks twined together into a structure shaped like a double helix. Portions of the DNA (genes) are used as patterns from which a simpler form, RNA, is constructed. RNA consists of just a single strand of chemical building blocks, very similar to one of the strands of DNA.

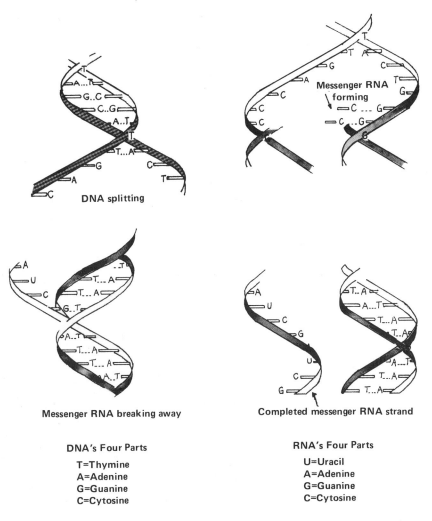

DNA splitting

Messenger RNA
\ forming

Messenger RNA breaking away

Completed messenger RNA strand

DNA's Four Parts

T=Thymine
A=Adenine
G=Guanine
C=Cytosine

RNA's Four Parts

U=Uracil
A=Adenine
G=Guanine
C=Cytosine

Messenger RNA is formed according to the pattern spelled out on the DNA strands.

Reading off the code in the sequence of RNA building blocks, the cell constructs proteins, which build up the cell's structures and conduct its chemical reactions. The normal translation process goes from DNA to RNA to protein. But retroviruses don't have any DNA. Their hereditary information is coded in a single strand of RNA. Inside a cell, the retrovirus makes the normal process run backward: Its RNA is used as a pattern for making a DNA copy, which then acts like a gene to produce new virus materials.

There was evidence that in AIDS patients, something selectively attacked the T cells—in fact, one specific kind of T cells, the helper cells. In a healthy person the helper T cells outnumber the suppressor T cells by about two to one. In an AIDS patient the ratio is reversed, and in advanced cases there are practically no helper T cells at all. Gallo reasoned that the AIDS virus must be one that homes in on T cells, like HTLV-I, only it destroys the cells instead of causing them to multiply. Perhaps it was a variation of the HTLV family. (Two types of cancer-causing HTLV viruses had already been found.)

There are tests for retroviruses. In forcing the cell to produce a DNA copy of its RNA, a retrovirus uses an enzyme called reverse transcriptase. Tests to detect the presence of reverse transcriptase are thus tests for retroviruses.

Gallo decided to isolate T cells from AIDS patients, grow them in culture dishes so that he would have enough material to work with, and then test them for retroviruses. It was a good idea, but unfortunately it didn't work. The T cells failed to grow. On dish after dish they just died out. Gallo put the specimens away in the deep-freeze, hoping to try again later, when better culture techniques were worked out. Meanwhile, his team published some articles to tell other scientists about their experiments.

In France, another research team was working on a similar theory, but with differences in some key steps in the experiments. They reasoned that by the time a patient has AIDS, the virus has killed most of the T cells and gradually disappears itself, because it has nowhere left to grow. But for each AIDS patient there are about ten people suffering from a condition called lymphadenopathy syndrome or ARC (AIDS-related complex). These people complain of swollen lymph nodes and fever. They are not seriously ill, but they don't feel completely well, either. Some people with ARC (doctors aren't sure yet exactly how many) will eventually develop a full-blown case of AIDS, some will get better, and some will stay about the same.

Dr. Willy Rozenbaum, a physician treating AIDS patients at the Hôpital La Pitié-Salpétrière in Paris, reasoned that the AIDS virus would be more likely to be found in a patient with ARC, whose helper T cells had not been wiped out. He took a lymph-node sample from one of his patients and sent it to the Institut Pasteur for testing. There a team headed by Dr. Luc Montagnier isolated T cells and cultured them for several days (another change in the procedure: Gallo's team had cultured their T cells for several weeks). When Montagnier tested the T cells for reverse transcriptase, he found a considerable amount of retrovirus activity. The excited French researchers placed a call to Bethesda, asking for a set of materials to test for HTLV-I. Gallo's team sent the test kit over right away, but the French lymphadenopathy virus did not react with it.

Tests continued, and the French team tried to isolate the virus and grow enough of it for further work. They were able to take a picture of the virus with an electron microscope. Like Gallo's team, however, they found that the original T cells died out when attempts were made to culture them for longer than several days.

The French researchers succeeded in transferring the virus to batches of fresh T cells; but with each transfer the virus weakened, and they were unable to grow enough of it to study its structure. Still, they had found a retrovirus in helper T cells from an ARC patient, and they published a report about their findings in the prestigious journal *Science* in May of 1983. In their first report the French scientists said that the virus appeared to be a member of the HTLV group (though not HTLV-I), but as they continued their studies they became more and more convinced that it did not belong to that group after all. They gave it a new name, LAV, or lymphadenopathy-associated virus.

Meanwhile work in Bethesda continued, and Gallo's research team made an important breakthrough. They produced a special line of T cells that would continue to grow, even when infected with the AIDS virus. Now they started pulling out the frozen samples they had stored and began retesting them. Tests for HTLV-I were negative, but a new retrovirus was isolated and grown in substantial amounts in cell cultures. Antibodies against it were produced to be used in tests of patients' blood and tissues.

Next the researchers tested their antibody test. Dr. James Curran, head of the AIDS task force in the CDC in Atlanta, sent over 205 blood samples. Some were from AIDS patients, some from patients with hepatitis, and some were from healthy volunteers. The CDC didn't tell the Gallo team which samples were which, but the new antibody test identified nearly every one correctly. Gallo named the new virus HTLV-III, and in late April of 1984, Secretary of Health and Human Services Margaret Heckler triumphantly announced at a press conference that the cause of AIDS had been discovered, and a test for it had been devised. "Today we add another miracle to the long honor roll of American medicine and science," she stated, a remark that made the French furious, since their research team had announced the isolation of the AIDS virus a full year before the report on Gallo's work was published.

Gallo justifies his claim to the discovery by the fact that the French researchers had not demonstrated that their virus was actually the cause of AIDS. His team's painstaking work, on the other hand, had not only conclusively linked the virus with AIDS but also yielded a test for it. He pointed to scientific notebooks dating back to November of 1982, showing findings similar to those the French reported in May of 1983, and commented that his team hadn't considered those results significant enough to publish.

Since then, the American team has determined the gene structure of the HTLV-III virus, and French team has determined the gene structure of LAV. These findings and other tests have shown that the two are minor variations of the same virus, but the two teams cling stubbornly to their own names for the virus. The Americans have changed the meaning of HTLV to human T-lymphotropic virus, since HTLV-III does not cause leukemia. The French sometimes use a modified meaning of LAV: lymphadenopathy-AIDS virus. Others have suggested alternative names, such as ARV—AIDS-related virus or AIDS-associated retrovirus—and HIV-I—human immunodeficiency virus-1, devised by an international committee of scientists. As the rest of the scientific community takes sides, the debate for priority continues.

There is more than just glory at stake. The scientists are disputing not only the virus's name but its nature as well. Gallo's team says that the AIDS virus is a member of the HTLV family, while the French researchers claim it belongs to a different family, the lentiviruses ("slow viruses"), other members of which cause serious blood and brain diseases in

animals. The latest findings on the structure of the virus seem to give some support to that claim, as do observations that in addition to attacking helper T cells, the AIDS virus also attacks and destroys brain tissue. Knowing which family the virus belongs to can make a big difference in researchers' attempts to produce treatments for the disease and vaccines to prevent it.

Other lines of research are casting some light on where the AIDS virus came from and how it burst onto the scene so suddenly. Harvard University researcher Myron Essex and his coworkers have found antibodies to an AIDS-like virus in green monkeys from Central Africa. About 70 percent of the monkeys tested had the antibodies in their blood, although they were healthy. In their homes in the African jungles, green monkeys live close to humans and often bite people. AIDS is a serious health problem in parts of Kenya, Uganda, and Tanzania and has been for some time. Some researchers have reported that frozen blood samples taken from people in Uganda in the early 1970s tested positive for AIDS antibodies, though others have challenged these findings.

Essex speculates that sometime in the past twenty to forty years, a form of AIDS virus spread from green monkeys to people living in Central Africa. Other viruses, such as the jungle yellow-fever virus, have made a similar jump from animals to humans. Why this happened so recently, when monkeys and humans have been living side by side in Africa for many thousands of years, is a puzzle. Perhaps a mutation—a change in the hereditary makeup—made the virus better suited to infecting humans. Studies have shown that the AIDS virus does indeed mutate, even more readily and rapidly than the flu virus, whose frequent changes make it necessary to produce new flu vaccines every few years.

From Africa the virus seems to have spread to Haiti and to the United States. Public health experts are not sure how

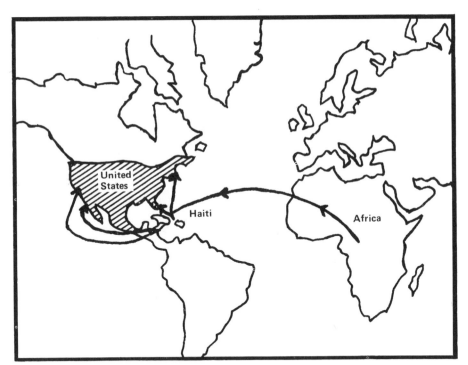

AIDS is believed to have spread from Africa to Haiti and the United States.

this happened, but it is known that several thousand Haitians lived in Kinshasa, Zaire, from the early 1960s to the mid-1970s, and then most of them moved to the United States and Europe. Another speculation is that American gays vacationing in Haiti or in Africa may have helped to carry the disease back to New York and California, from which it has been spreading to the rest of the country.

The origin of the AIDS virus and the history of its spread through the world have become sensitive political issues. Nations of Central Africa resent the implication that they are somehow to blame for the new medical threat to the world and deny that AIDS originated in Africa. But the point of efforts to trace the history of AIDS is not to cast blame on Africans, Haitians, gays, or any other particular group. Such studies are aimed at finding out more about the disease and how it is spread so that researchers can find ways to prevent and cure it.

4

AIDS Facts and Myths

The disease is so new that even the experts don't have all the answers, so it is not surprising that most people have a lot of questions about AIDS and a lot of mistaken ideas about this deadly threat. But each day important decisions have to be made on how to deal with AIDS and the people who suffer from it. Local, state, and national governments must decide whether new laws and policies are needed to protect the public at large and to safeguard the rights of AIDS sufferers. The military services, insurance companies, and various other organizations have their own policy decisions to make. Even individuals find themselves faced with difficult choices, as they must weigh the risks of personal danger against the needs of the victims—some of whom may be friends or loved ones. To make intelligent decisions we need facts, not myths.

What is AIDS?

AIDS is a serious viral disease that damages the body's natural immune defenses. The virus that causes it, called HTLV-III, LAV, HIV-I, or ARV, invades the type of lymphocytes called helper T cells, turns them into virus factories, and eventually kills them. Without helper T cells to recognize invading microbes and stimulate B cells to produce antibodies against them, the AIDS victim is vulnerable to many serious infections that would not be dangerous for a person with a normally functioning immune system. Such rare opportunistic infections as *Pneumocystis carinii* pneumonia and a type of cancer called Kaposi's sarcoma serve as "markers" for AIDS infection and are often the cause of death. In addition to attacking T cells, the AIDS virus can also attack and destroy brain cells, producing serious brain damage.

AIDS is a major health problem. Although its numbers are still relatively small (a total of about twenty-two thousand cases reported in the United States as of mid-1986), the totals have more than doubled each year since the disease appeared. The actual totals may be even larger, since some doctors hesitate to report AIDS cases or list AIDS as the cause of death,

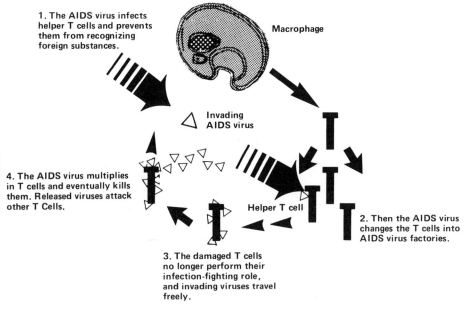

1. The AIDS virus infects helper T cells and prevents them from recognizing foreign substances.

Macrophage

Invading AIDS virus

4. The AIDS virus multiplies in T cells and eventually kills them. Released viruses attack other T Cells.

Helper T cell

2. Then the AIDS virus changes the T cells into AIDS virus factories.

3. The damaged T cells no longer perform their infection-fighting role, and invading viruses travel freely.

When the AIDS virus invades helper T cells, the normal immune defenses break down.

fearing that this might embarrass the victim's family or even cause discrimination against them.

Medical experts believe that for each AIDS patient there are ten more with ARC (AIDS-related complex), a milder condition in which the person has swollen lymph nodes, suffers from fevers and night sweats, and feels generally tired and ill. For each person with ARC or AIDS, there are about ten who have been exposed to the virus and carry antibodies to it in their blood. That means that more than a million people have already been exposed. Because the incubation period of AIDS (the time between exposure to the virus and the appearance of symptoms) is very long—up to seven years or more—nobody knows yet how many of the people with AIDS antibodies will eventually develop the disease. Some experts estimate the total will be about 5 to 10 percent; others say 10 to 20 percent.

AIDS is a worldwide problem. So far, the largest number of cases by far has been reported in the United States, which has more AIDS victims than all the countries in the rest of the

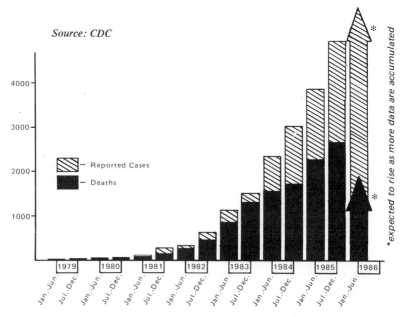

Reported AIDS cases and deaths in the United States have continued to rise.

world combined. However, substantial numbers of cases have also appeared in various countries of South America (Brazil is second in the world) and Europe (France, West Germany, and Britain have the highest numbers of AIDS cases among the European countries). Tiny Haiti ranks fourth in the world in number of AIDS victims, and the disease has also spread to Canada and Mexico, the countries of the Middle East, and as far as Japan, Australia, and New Zealand. The Iron Curtain countries do not admit officially to having significant numbers of AIDS cases, but their public-health officials are concerned about the problem. In the Soviet Union, for example, where homosexual activity is punishable by up to five years in prison and only a dozen AIDS cases had been reported by mid-1986, the head of Moscow's immunology institute has called AIDS "an urgent medical problem." Major clinics are being set up in the USSR to study immune deficiencies, and nationwide blood-donor screening has been started. AIDS is a serious health problem in Africa, where the disease is called "slim disease," because of the severe weight loss it produces, or "the horror." In the "AIDS belt" in Central Africa, as much as 10 to 20 percent of the adult population may already have been exposed to the virus. The exact numbers of AIDS cases in Africa are uncertain. Not all cases are reported to the World Health Organization (WHO) Collaborating Center on AIDS, and because the assortment of opportunistic infections that strike African victims is somewhat different from those that are seen in American and European patients, many AIDS cases may not be recognized. In mid-1986, WHO estimated that the total of AIDS cases in Africa may actually have passed fifty thousand, with between one and two million symptomless carriers of the virus.

AIDS is not a "gay plague." Although about 73 percent of the victims in the United States are sexually active homosexual and bisexual men, another 17 percent are intravenous drug abusers (including both men and women), and the rest fall into various other categories. Growing numbers of them are young children. In Africa, where the disease first appeared, AIDS affects about equal numbers of men and women and does not appear to have any particular connection with homosexuality.

What are the symptoms of AIDS?

The first signs of AIDS may be rather mild and vague. Feelings of tiredness and an unexplained loss of weight may go on for months. The person may be feverish and achy and wake up sweating at night. "Swollen glands" (lymph nodes) are a typical symptom. Headaches, difficulty in concentrating, and mild feelings of depression are also common signs. All these symptoms could be explained by a case of flu or some other common infection, and many patients tend to ignore them, denying that they might be a sign of something more serious.

Typically, it is the more acute symptoms of an opportunistic infection that send the AIDS patient to the doctor or hospital. A persistent cough, increasing difficulties in breathing, and high fevers are symptoms of pneumocystis pneumonia. Other infections may produce such symptoms as epilepsy-like seizures, severe prolonged diarrhea, or fungus growths in the mouth and throat. The appearance of purplish spots on the skin is a sign of Kaposi's sarcoma. Doctors in New Jersey and Florida have reported that tuberculosis is often found in AIDS patients, although this disease is not yet included in the CDC's list of opportunistic infections typical of AIDS.

When the AIDS virus attacks the brain, the victim has increasing difficulties in thinking and concentrating. Speech and movements are slowed. Memory losses develop, and there is a progressive loss of mental and physical abilities.

Because the symptoms of AIDS are often so similar to those of other diseases, doctors use a variety of tests to determine damage to the immune system and the presence of AIDS antibodies.

How do you catch AIDS?

Can you catch AIDS by shaking hands with someone who has the disease? Or kissing? By sharing food? Or using an AIDS patient's towel? Can you catch AIDS from a toilet seat? Or by being sneezed on?

When people find out that AIDS is a contagious disease caused by a virus, their natural reaction is to think you can catch it just as easily as you can catch a cold. Fortunately, it's not that easy. The AIDS virus is rather delicate. Although it can survive outside the body for up to a week or more, it is deactivated by heat and is killed by common detergents and even hand soap. All the evidence so far indicates that AIDS cannot be transmitted by casual, everyday contacts such as touching an AIDS patient, talking, even eating together. Family members who live with an AIDS patient remain free of the disease, unless they engage in sexual activity together.

Hospital workers who have cared for AIDS patients for years, feeding them, bathing them, and cleaning away their body wastes, typically do not even carry AIDS antibodies in their blood. The few exceptions have been cases in which blood or tissue from an AIDS patient has been accidentally introduced into the medical worker's body—for example, by being jabbed with a needle that was used to collect the patient's blood.

Both the blood and semen of AIDS patients contain the virus. Smaller concentrations of AIDS virus have also been found in saliva and in tears, and doctors believe they are probably present in all the patient's body fluids. But there have been no confirmed cases of transmission of AIDS by saliva or tears. Medical specialists believe the virus concentrations in these fluids may be too low to produce infection. All the ways of catching AIDS that have been discovered so far involve either sexual activity or a transfer of contaminated blood.

It is not only the actual AIDS patients who are contagious. Anyone who has been exposed to the virus may be able to transmit it to others, even though he or she does not have symptoms of the disease. Probably most people suffering from AIDS now were infected by people who felt perfectly healthy when they transmitted the disease and had no idea that they were a danger to others. Since it takes from six months to five years or more after exposure for the first symptoms of AIDS to appear, there is a very long danger period in which carriers of the virus may not realize they need to take special precautions. Tests for AIDS antibodies can detect an AIDS virus infection much sooner, however.

The rapid spread of AIDS through the American gay community has been vivid evidence of the danger of infection through certain types of sexual activity. Anal intercourse is believed to be the most dangerous, because it often produces small tears in the delicate lining of the rectum. The AIDS virus can pass from infected semen into the bloodstream of the sex partner through these small breaks in the lining. Theoretically, the virus could also enter the bloodstream through a cut or sore in the mouth during oral sex, but it has not yet been established definitely that this kind of sexual activity presents a risk.

For a time, medical researchers thought the virus might not be transmitted by vaginal intercourse, the most common type of heterosexual sex activity. The lining of the vagina is well adapted to resist tears and abrasions, and germ-killing secretions provide additional protection. Now there is considerable evidence that AIDS can be transmitted by vaginal intercourse. Wives of AIDS patients have contracted the disease, and some cases have even been reported in which women who became pregnant by artificial insemination have caught AIDS from semen donated by carriers of the disease. The virus is believed to be transmitted more easily from an infected man to a woman than from an infected woman to a man, but this is still being studied. Scientists in Boston and San Francisco reported in March 1986 that they had found the AIDS virus in vaginal secretions, which could be a means of transmitting the virus from an infected woman to her partner during intercourse. Homosexual activity among women does not transmit AIDS: The disease does not occur among lesbians.

The second largest group of Americans at risk of catching AIDS is drug addicts who take drugs by injection. It isn't the drugs that increase their risk, but rather the needles used for the injections. Addicts often reuse needles and share them with others. If one of the people sharing a needle carries the AIDS virus, traces of contaminated blood on the needle can transmit the disease to anyone who uses the same needle afterward. Some doctors and dentists also reuse needles for injections, but they wash and sterilize them by heat treatments before each reuse and thus kill any lingering viruses or other germs.

In New York City, which has the largest number of AIDS cases in the nation, laws make it illegal to possess a hypodermic needle without a doctor's prescription. These laws represent an attempt to prevent drug abuse by making it more difficult for addicts to use injectable drugs. Such restrictions have not been very effective in stopping the spread of drug abuse—people who buy illegal drugs can also buy (or steal) illegal needles. Publicity about the link between contaminated needles and AIDS has resulted in a thriving black market in hypodermic needles. Some drug dealers rinse off used needles, reseal the packages, and sell them as new.

Meanwhile, in New York City, about a third of the new cases of AIDS are occurring among current or former drug addicts—twice the national average. In 1985 Dr. David Sencer, the New York City Health Commissioner, proposed that needles be sold over the counter to help cut down the dangers of shared needles. "It's one way to stop transmission," Sencer pointed out. "People don't become addicted to needles. They become addicted to drugs." Sencer's suggestion was rejected by the city's mayor, district attorneys, and the National Institute on Drug Abuse.

AIDS can occur not only in drug abusers but also in former addicts. People who successfully conquered the habit as long as five or six years before and are finally getting their lives straightened out—working in good jobs, marrying and raising families—suddenly are struck by this life-threatening disease. Another tragedy is that children of drug addicts or former addicts are being born with AIDS. The virus can pass from an infected mother's bloodstream through the placenta into her unborn child's body. Drug addicts may also be helping to spread AIDS into the general population. A drug habit is very expensive to maintain. Many drug users work as prostitutes to support their habit, and they can pass the AIDS virus to their customers during sexual activity.

About 1 percent of the AIDS cases reported so far have occurred in hemophiliacs. These unfortunate people suffer from a hereditary disease in which the blood lacks some of the key factors that help blood to clot. Without treatment, many of them would lead very restricted lives, in constant danger of bleeding to death from a minor cut or a simple dental operation. Treatments with blood factors obtained from the blood of donors can help these people to live normal lives. Each dose of blood factors is concentrated from the blood of up to twenty thousand donors. That means that in one year, a hemophiliac is exposed to more than a million different blood samples. If just a small percentage of these samples is contaminated with the AIDS virus, that is enough to transmit the disease. The occurrence of AIDS in hemophiliacs who were neither homosexual nor drug abusers was one of the first bits of evidence suggesting that the disease was transmitted by a virus. Now that the danger has been recognized, the screening of donor blood for AIDS antibodies and sterilization procedures to kill viruses that may slip through should prevent new cases of blood-transmitted AIDS in hemophilia sufferers. But such cases will continue to appear for at least the next few years, because of the long incubation period of the virus.

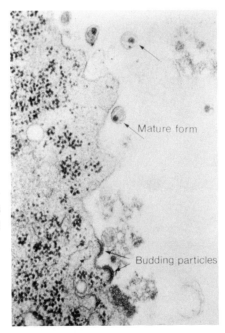

Magnified view of AIDS virus found in a hemophilia patient who developed AIDS.

Early in 1983, Dr. Joseph Bove, chairman of the American Association of Blood Banks committee on transfusion-transmitted diseases and a professor of laboratory medicine at Yale University, stated, "The evidence is that ordinary blood transfusions are not transmitting AIDS. Twenty million people have been transfused, and some must have gotten blood from donors with AIDS. But we don't see an epidemic of AIDS spread by blood." Other medical experts objected that Dr. Bove was not taking the long incubation period of the disease into account. They predicted that a growing number of AIDS cases would be reported among people whose only possible exposure to the disease was through blood transfusion. Unfortunately, their predictions proved all too accurate, and concern about the safety of the blood supply grew.

Blood banks began asking male homosexuals to refrain from donating blood, even if they appeared to be healthy. But some kind of reliable screening method was needed. At the April 1984 press conference at which the identification of the AIDS virus was announced, Health Secretary Margaret Heckler promised that blood-screening tests would be available in record time. Within nine months they were ready, and medical companies mass-produced kits in crash programs. Some medical experts feared that with that kind of rushing, the tests might not be reliable enough, but experience in using them has shown that they are 99.8 percent accurate.

United States blood banks now routinely screen donated blood for AIDS antibodies; samples that test positive are rejected and are not passed on to patients. Special centers are also being set up where people in high-risk groups, such as sexually active homosexual and bisexual men, prostitutes, and drug abusers, can have their blood checked if they are worried about the possibility of having been exposed to the virus. The use of such facilities may help to ease fears that people in high-risk groups might volunteer to give blood in order to be tested, and a few contaminated samples might slip through. As an additional precaution, the FDA has recommended for several years that blood banks request a man not to donate blood if he has had any sexual experience with another man since 1977. (People in high-risk groups should also refrain from donating organs for transplants or semen for artificial insemination.) Although there shold be few if any new AIDS cases resulting from blood transfusions since the testing programs were set up, as with hemophiliacs, there are still many people who have already been exposed and will develop the disease in the years to come.

Medical experts believe that various contributing factors may help to determine which people get AIDS after being exposed to the virus. There is evidence that heredity may make some people more susceptible to the diseases that commonly accompany AIDS, such as Kaposi's sarcoma. Another important factor is a history of other infections that have weakened the body's defenses. It is possible that certain specific infections such as cytomegalovirus (CMV), hepatitis, or African swine fever may act as cofactors, aiding the AIDS virus to gain a foothold. Repeated exposure to the AIDS virus itself also seems to be a contributing factor. The use of inhalant drugs, such as nitrite poppers, which may lower the immune defenses, also has not been ruled out as a possible AIDS cofactor.

Researchers still are not sure how many of the people infected with the virus will ultimately develop ARC or AIDS, but they hope that large-scale studies of gay men and other volunteers from high-risk groups will provide some answers. Such studies have already suggested that people with positive antibody tests and very low levels of helper T cells seem to be much more likely to develop AIDS than those who are infected but have normal numbers of helper T cells. These and other correlations that are gradually emerging may eventually yield tests to determine the risk of developing AIDS.

Researchers are especially interested in finding out what factors promote the spread of AIDS in Africa, where the disease affects equal numbers of men and women. Both sexual transmission and exchanges of contaminated blood seem to be involved. Prostitutes with many sex partners are common, and because of limited budgets, health workers often reuse needles to inject drugs and vaccines. Needles are also reused and shared by the people of the region for tattooing and ritual scarring.

Similar contributing factors and transmission routes probably account for the high AIDS disease rate in Haiti. For a time, the CDC considered Haitian immigrants who had entered the United States since 1978 to be a major risk group for AIDS, but that is no longer the case. It was decided that since Haitians catch AIDS in the same ways as other people—mainly through sexual contacts and the transfer of contaminated blood by shared needles—it was unfair and discriminatory to single them out as a special risk group.

Drug addiction and promiscuous sexual activity are also believed to be the causes of a curious cluster of AIDS cases in Belle Glade, Florida, a town that has the highest percentage of AIDS cases in the United States. Some health workers think mosquitoes breeding in local swampy areas may be helping to spread the virus, but CDC experts say there is no evidence that this virus can be carried by mosquitoes.

Thus, in all the cases studied, the AIDS virus has been spread in one of the following ways:

• intimate sexual contact in which body fluids are transferred from one partner to the other;

• transfer of infected blood by unsterilized, reused needles;

• blood transfusions or the use of blood factors made from contaminated donor blood;

• passage of the virus from the bloodstream of an infected mother into the body of her unborn child.

Is it safe to get a blood transfusion?

The test now being used in the United States to screen samples of donor blood for the AIDS virus is an ELISA test. The abbreviation stands for enzyme-linked immuno-sorbent assay. This test is highly accurate, but it does give some "false positives"—results that indicate the presence of virus antibodies when they are not really there. Questions about the accuracy of a positive test can usually be cleared up by simply repeating the test. Or a more complicated and expensive test called the Western blot test can be used to double check the result. New tests now being developed, based on the use of gene-splicing techniques, may soon be used as backups to eliminate the false positives. Experience has shown that even with the current tests, confirmed positive reports are about 99.8 percent accurate, and negative results are virtually 100 percent accurate.

In Great Britain a similar blood-screening program has been set up, using a radioimmunoassay test, which is also based on the reaction of AIDS antibodies in a blood sample with purified AIDS virus. A new kind of test recently developed by British researchers at Cambridge University is highly accurate, fast, and cheap. Instead of purified virus, the new test uses virus-infected T cells that have been treated to kill the virus.

Harvard researcher David Archibald reports that his group has developed a highly accurate test for AIDS antibodies in saliva. The results check perfectly with blood tests, and saliva tests could be developed for large-scale screening.

Now that blood banks are screening donor blood with tests such as these, medical experts say that our blood supply is safe. However, some doctors add a note of caution. They point out that it takes two to eight weeks after exposure to the

AIDS virus before detectable antibodies appear in a person's blood—and some infected people never produce antibodies at all. So a person who has recently been exposed may be infectious but still pass an AIDS blood-screening test. That is why blood banks request people to refrain from giving blood if they are in a high-risk group for AIDS. With these precautions, there is now only a very small risk of getting AIDS from a blood transfusion—far smaller than the risks to life and health from *not* having a needed blood transfusion.

The risk will be even smaller when the next generation of AIDS tests is perfected. These new tests detect the actual AIDS virus, not antibodies against it. The reason such tests had not been devised before is that the virus is found in only a small number of white blood cells, perhaps one in 500,000. A blood sample does not contain enough of the virus-infected cells to be detected. In mid-1986, Du Pont began marketing a radioimmunoassay test kit designed to detect a protein from the inner core of the AIDS virus. This test is faster and more sensitive than the reverse transcriptase tests that researchers had been using to detect the presence of the AIDS virus. Since it measures the actual amount of the core protein, the Du Pont test can be used to determine the degree of viral activity in the infected cells. The test kit is being sold only for research purposes, though, not to screen blood samples. The biotechnology firms Cetus and Enzo are working on AIDS virus tests to be used in screening. These tests use a gene probe, a chain of DNA that homes in on a portion of the virus's genes, which have been copied out in the form of DNA and attached to the white cell's chromosomes. The probe has a chemical or radioactive "tag" that can be spotted by test instruments. The new tests use different approaches to compensate for the very small amounts of virus nucleic acid. Enzo's gene probe contains an especially high-powered radioisotope that sends out a strong signal. Cetus uses chemical methods to multiply the target gene into about a million copies so that it can be detected more easily.

Even a very small risk seems too much for some people, who are having pints of their own blood frozen and stored in case they may need an emergency transfusion at some time in the future. The stored blood is good for three years. The matter of blood transfusions is very serious to many people who are haunted by the widely publicized cases of children who contracted AIDS from blood transfusions, or men infected by contaminated blood products who passed the disease on to their wives. One woman scheduled for surgery even brought a lawsuit seeking to compel the hospital to use only the blood she herself had donated in advance.

To keep things in perspective, we should recall that even before blood-screening tests were in use, the number of AIDS cases resulting from blood transfusions amounted to only a few hundred out of the tens of *millions* of blood transfusions that are given each year.

One final note about blood transfusions: You can't catch AIDS by *donating* blood. When the dangers of AIDS from blood transfusions began to be published, blood banks observed a disturbing drop in the number of blood donors. People were reacting with fear to a misunderstanding of the situation. When blood is collected from a donor, a disposable needle is used. It is thrown away afterward, so there is no chance of coming in contact with anybody else's blood. Giving blood is completely safe.

Is AIDS always fatal?

In a recent TV report about AIDS, a medical expert commented, "AIDS is always fatal." Yet articles about the disease sometimes mention a "mortality rate of about 50 percent." It seems rather confusing.

Actually, there is some support for each of these conflicting statements, but neither tells the whole story. Nobody knows all the facts yet, but what we do know is this: Doctors are trying a variety of drugs and other treatments for AIDS, but so far there is no cure for the disease. Many patients respond well to treatments for opportunistic diseases such as pneumocystis pneumonia or Kaposi's sarcoma and recover from them. But the patient's immune system does not recover. It is still damaged, and the patient is still vulnerable to the next infection that comes along. Close to 90 percent of AIDS patients die within two years after the disease is diagnosed. And if you look at the history of AIDS, going back to its first appearance in the United States, you'll find that at any particular time about half of the people who have been diagnosed as suffering from AIDS have died. That is what is meant by the "50 percent mortality rate."

Those statistics seem depressing. The bright side is that some of the earliest AIDS patients are still alive. They have recovered from the bouts of pneumonia or cancer that threatened to kill them, they have regained the weight they lost, and they are now apparently free of illness. Their immune defenses have not recovered, and neither they nor their doctors know how long they will continue in good health. But they are alive and hopeful.

How is AIDS treated?

The dramatic announcement in 1985 that movie star Rock Hudson was suffering from AIDS focused attention not only on the disease but also on the ways it is currently being

Rock Hudson with Doris Day shortly before it was announced that he had AIDS. His gaunt appearance shocked everyone.

treated. Hudson had gone to Paris to be treated with HPA-23, an experimental drug that was not available in the United States.

Medical researchers are hard at work on developing a vaccine to prevent AIDS and various ways to treat people who already have the disease. But there are no cures yet, and in the meantime doctors must do the best they can with the treatments that are available. Their efforts are focused in several main directions: treating the life-threatening infections as each one comes up; attacking the AIDS virus with antiviral drugs; and trying to strengthen the body's damaged immune defenses.

The discouraging thing about treating the opportunistic diseases that accompany AIDS is that a patient may seem to respond well but then relapse or fall prey to another illness. Pneumocystis pneumonia is particularly dangerous. Patients with Kaposi's sarcoma show a somewhat better rate of survival.

Most of the antiviral drugs being tried against AIDS are still highly experimental, and some of them have potentially dangerous side effects. The French drug HPA-23, which contains tungsten and antimony, works by blocking the enzyme reverse transcriptase and thus preventing the virus from reproducing, but there are questions about how effective it is in treating actual AIDS patients. Other antiviral drugs being tested against AIDS include AZT (azidothymidine), foscarnet, ribavirin, and deoxycytidine. These drugs interfere with various parts of the virus life cycle. A combination of lipids called AL 721 appears to inactivate the AIDS virus by stripping cholesterol out of its outer envelope. The antiviral drug isoprinosine is believed to work mainly by bolstering the immune system.

Natural body substances are also being tested: interferon, the natural body defense against invading viruses that helps to keep them in check while antibodies and other specific defenses are being readied; interleukin-2, which boosts the activity of killer T cells; and met-enkephalin, a natural brain chemical that has been found to increase the numbers of T cells in AIDS and cancer patients and makes the T cells more responsive to interleukin-2. Transplanting bone marrow from healthy donors is another approach designed to restore the body's immune defenses.

The development and testing of new drugs against AIDS have sparked fierce debates about some thorny ethical questions. Often the beliefs and practices of scientists are pitted against their own sympathies and the anguish of AIDS patients and their friends and relatives, who argue that traditional methods are simply too slow when so many people are dying. Should experimental drugs be provided freely for all the AIDS patients who would like to try them, or should their use be restricted to small numbers of patients in carefully controlled test programs? Traditional methods provide for years of tests, first on animals and then on small groups of carefully observed human patients to determine whether the drugs are safe and effective. But with a disease in which most of the patients have died within two years of being diagnosed, following the traditional rules of research means that potentially life-saving drugs must be denied to thousands.

The Food and Drug Administration (FDA), which approves and licenses drugs for use in the United States, has set up some "fast-track" machinery for speeded-up testing of important new drugs and the "compassionate use" of drugs for particularly deadly diseases before they have completed all the testing necessary for full approval. (When a patient is dying, what difference does it make if a drug that might save his or her life has some long-term side effects?) In practice, however, these procedures do not always work effectively.

The drug isoprinosine, for example, is currently on sale for the treatment of viral diseases in about seventy countries around the world, but as of early 1986 it had not been approved in the United States. The FDA authorized compassionate use of the drug for AIDS patients, but the manufacturer was reluctant to release the drug for wide use on that basis for several reasons. Drugs distributed for compassionate use cannot be sold for profit, which means that the company producing them cannot cover the huge costs of developing and producing the drug. The manufacturer of isoprinosine was doubtful that it could meet the demand that might result if the drug were made available to all, and it was feared that wide and uncontrolled use of the drug might hinder the clinical tests designed to win approval for its sale. In addition, it has not yet been established whether isoprinosine is really effective against AIDS. Some researchers believe that it will prove effective in ARC, which damages the immune system only slightly. In patients with fully developed AIDS, doctors fear it might actually stimulate the spread of the virus and make the patient worse.

Meanwhile, isoprinosine and another antiviral drug, ribavirin, were widely publicized, especially in the gay press, and a sort of underground testing program developed. The drugs were sold legally in Mexico, and United States AIDS patients living close to the border began taking isoprinosine and ribavirin on their own. Supplies of the drugs were smuggled across the border and distributed to other parts of the United States, where they were sold to AIDS patients and their doctors, often at huge markups. Sympathetic doctors monitored the treatments and reported that their patients' conditions stabilized or improved, with no new opportunistic infections developing. ARC patients showed some recovery of the immune system, although they remained positive for the virus antibodies.

In December 1985, the FDA approved the use of ribavirin against respiratory syncytial virus, a common infection in children. This meant that United States doctors could now legally prescribe the drug for their AIDS patients, too. Early in 1986, approval was granted for clinical trials of a combination of ribavirin and isoprinosine for AIDS patients. This FDA action represented an important shortcut in normal testing procedures. Only a few months before, some medical researchers were arguing that the drugs needed to be tested separately first, in order to understand their effects, even though they conceded that the drugs might be much more effective working together than they would be alone. Isoprinosine helps to boost the immune system generally, while ribavirin has been found to inhibit the AIDS virus.

Together with drugs and other medical therapies, important procedures in the treatment of AIDS patients are counseling, to help them cope with their own emotional reactions and fears, and practical help in coping with the problems of day-to-day living. Finding out that one is suffering from a disease that is fatal can be devastating, especially when a person is still relatively young, as most AIDS patients are. The knowledge that catching the disease may have resulted from behavior that could have been avoided—and behavior that many people disapprove of—can add a tremendous burden of guilt. "God is punishing me for being gay," one AIDS patient remarked to his doctor.

The fatigue and general ill health that the disease produces can also have a depressing effect. Hospital expenses can wipe out a person's savings. Treatment costs average close to $100,000 per AIDS patient! Lack of understanding and support by panicky family and friends (or former friends) can be just as devastating as the medical dangers. Yet many studies have shown that a person's attitude can affect the workings of the immune system. Feelings of loneliness, despair, and helplessness actually make the body's defenses less effective, while feelings of hope can help the immune system to work better. An AIDS patient's immune system needs all the help it can get. AIDS support groups, such as the one sponsored by the Gay Men's Health Crisis in New York City, are helping to counter AIDS patients' feelings of isolation and helplessness. They provide discussion groups where patients and their family members or friends can voice their feelings and learn to cope with them, stressing positive attitudes. Buddy programs assign a volunteer to befriend an AIDS patient, bringing needed human contacts in addition to helping with practical chores like shopping, cooking, and cleaning. For many AIDS patients this friendship and support makes dying a little easier to bear; for some it provides new hope for living.

How can people avoid getting AIDS?

Even though a vaccine for AIDS has not yet been produced, the disease is preventable. People can greatly reduce their chances of contracting AIDS by following some commonsense rules, based on the ways the disease is transmitted.

First of all, the danger of getting AIDS provides a very good argument for knowing a person very well before deciding to have an intimate sexual relationship, and limiting your sex partners—preferably to one person, who also agrees that a one-to-one relationship is the most prudent choice. Health specialists recommend prudence in sexual practices, too. The use of condoms can help to avoid the exchange of body fluids that might transmit the AIDS virus. Water-based lubricants can help prevent tears in the lining of the rectum through which viruses could enter the bloodstream. Nonoxynol-9, a sperm-killing ingredient in many commercial spermicides and lubricants, has been found to kill AIDS viruses in a test tube and might also help to lower the risk of transmitting the disease by sexual activity. As for kissing; a casual kiss is probably safe enough, but since the AIDS virus has been found in saliva—even though there is no evidence that saliva can transmit the disease—it might be prudent to avoid deep open-mouth kissing.

There are plenty of good reasons besides AIDS to avoid becoming addicted to drugs or, if one is already addicted, to get into a treatment program and kick the habit as quickly as possible. Drug users can reduce their risk of catching AIDS by not sharing needles, but it is not always possible to be sure that a needle is uncontaminated to start with.

Avoid other situations where contaminated needles may be used, too. If you have your ears pierced or have acupuncture treatments, make sure the needles have been properly sterilized, not just rinsed off after the last use.

As for the blood transfusions, the risk is already extremely small. But it can be further minimized by arranging with the hospital to donate your own blood in advance when elective surgery is planned, to be used if a transfusion is needed.

Get enough sleep and eat sensibly. Studies suggest that people whose general health is good stand a better chance of fighting off the AIDS virus if they are exposed. Certain vitamins (A, C, and E) and minerals (selenium and zinc) can help to strengthen the immune system and provide protection against viruses and cancer; they may help in avoiding AIDS, too.

One thing you *don't* have to do to avoid catching AIDS is to avoid all contact with AIDS patients and people who might possibly be carrying the virus. AIDS is not spread by casual social contact. And AIDS patients—or people who fear they may become AIDS patients—need sensitive, caring friends who can help to bolster their feelings of self-worth and hope.

What should you do if you have AIDS, or if your blood has tested positive for AIDS antibodies?

First, don't panic. If you have been infected with the AIDS virus, that does not necessarily mean that you will develop the disease. Your chances of staying symptom-free will be improved if you follow the general rules for healthy living and avoid being reexposed to the AIDS virus or other viruses that can activate the immune system—in other words, take the same kind of precautions that people can use to avoid catching AIDS. In fact, there have been cases in which infected people who avoided reexposure to the virus not only stayed symptom free but eventually became seronegative—there was no longer any sign of AIDS antibodies in their blood.

If you have the disease, don't give up hope. The odds are bad, but there *are* AIDS patients who are beating them. New drugs and treatments now being developed in laboratories all over the world may bring the help you need, and meanwhile an optimistic outlook and an active interest in life can help your own body's defenses fight off the virus.

The question of pets may be a difficult one for AIDS patients and those infected with the virus. Both cats and dogs can carry numerous germs and parasites. A common example is *Toxoplasma gondii,* a microscopic parasite found in cat feces. Ordinarily these microorganisms do not infect humans or at most cause only a mild illness. In someone whose immune system is weakened, however, they can produce devastating opportunistic infections. Yet many studies have supported the idea that companion animals can have a positive effect on health, bringing love and comfort and helping to promote a wholesome outlook. If pets are a part of your life-style that you would not want to give up, some compromises would be prudent: Don't kiss your cat or dog on the mouth or rub noses with it or allow it to lick your face; don't sleep with a pet; and wear rubber gloves and wash thoroughly afterward if you have to change the cat litter or clean up after a dog.

An important thing to remember is that if you have been infected with the AIDS virus, even if you have no symptoms of disease, you may be able to infect others. If you are sexually active, avoid intimate contacts in which your body fluids are transferred to another person. Don't donate blood, share needles, or share a razor or toothbrush with anyone else. If your blood or other body fluids are spilled, the area should be thoroughly cleaned with a solution of household bleach, hydrogen peroxide, rubbing alcohol, or some other disinfectant. It is only fair to tell doctors, dentists, and other health-care workers who might come in contact with your body fluids that you are carrying the virus, so that they can take precautions against infection. Women carrying the AIDS virus have a 65 percent chance of passing the disease to an unborn child, so it is best for them to avoid getting pregant.

Read and learn as much about the disease as possible. With knowledge of AIDS facts, rather than myths, you can save yourself a lot of needless worry while keeping up to date on the best ways to protect yourself and others.

*   *   *

If you have any questions about AIDS and your own personal risks, there are some toll-free national AIDS hotlines that you can call:

• 1-800-342-AIDS, set up by the U.S. Public Health Service, gives a four-minute recording of current AIDS information, followed by a referral number (also 800) for people who have more specific questions.

• 1-800-221-7044, the AIDS 800 hotline, staffed by the National Gay/Lesbian Crisis Line, provides information and counseling for those with personal concerns about AIDS.

A listing of local agencies and hotlines can be found in the periodically updated *National Referral Directory of AIDS-Related Services,* prepared by the National Gay/Lesbian Crisis Line with the support of the U.S. Department of Health and Human Services. Local libraries can also supply numbers and addresses of organizations in your area that provide information and help.

5

The Young Victims

Some of the most tragic AIDS victims are children. Small but growing numbers of children suffer from the disease, and as AIDS spreads further into the general population, their numbers are expected to increase.

Most AIDS children were born with the disease, infected by the virus while they were still inside their mothers' bodies. Some are the children of drug abusers who contracted AIDS through shared needles. Some are the children of women who were infected by husbands who had had sexual contacts with gay men or who had been exposed to the virus through transfusions of blood or blood-clotting factors. The plight of these children is particularly sad because their parents, too, are ill— often too ill to care for them. Some have been placed in foster homes, but it is difficult to find people willing to take on the care of a foster child who is seriously ill. Some stay on in hospital wards because there is literally nowhere else for them to go.

Some of the young AIDS victims caught the disease after birth, through contaminated blood transfusions or treatments for hemophilia. The rate of AIDS cases from blood transfusions is higher in infants than in adults, perhaps because a baby's immune defenses are not yet fully developed.

Pediatricians like Dr. James Oleske of Newark Children's Hospital treat their tiny patients with nutritional supplements (fed intravenously or through tubes into the stomach, if necessary), shots of antibiotics and antibody-containing gamma globulin to strengthen their immune defenses, and plenty of hugs and tender loving care. These efforts are not enough to save some of the children. In addition to contracting a variety of opportunistic infections that bring one illness after another, children with AIDS are also more likely than adult patients to suffer from brain damage caused by the virus. About half of them have trouble speaking, walking, or seeing.

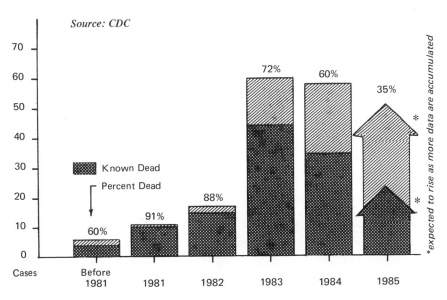

Pediatric AIDS: numbers of AIDS cases and deaths among children in the United States according to the year of diagnosis.

Caring for these tragic young AIDS patients is a terrible emotional drain on the doctors and nurses. "Seeing children die is very upsetting," says Oleske. "I went into pediatrics because I loved children. I wasn't emotionally equipped for AIDS. A lot of times I go home at night crying while driving on the parkway."

But there have been successes. Some of the young AIDS victims make what seems to be a full recovery. They are free of the recurring infections and healthy enough to live normal lives. But in some cases recovery has brought the AIDS children a different set of problems.

Should children with AIDS who have no current symptoms of illness be allowed to attend regular classes at school? Medical specialists at the federal Centers for Disease Control think they should. The CDC guidelines for the education of children infected with AIDS specify that decisions on the kind of schooling and care such children receive should be based on each child's behavior, development, and physical condition. A team including the child's physician, public-health workers, the child's parents or guardians, and representatives of the school should make the decision, taking into account the risks and benefits for the child and others. For most infected school-age children, they say, the benefits of going to school like other children outweigh the risks involved. The only restrictions they recommend are for those with open, oozing sores and for mentally or physically handicapped children, who may bite other people or drool, or who cannot control their bladders or bowels. Another special provision is that AIDS children cannot be given the immunizations with live vaccines that schools normally require. Their immune defenses are so poor that the vaccines can cause the disease they are supposed to prevent.

The guidelines seem clear, but decisions are made in the local school districts, and there have been heated disagreements about what is really best for AIDS children and for the children who would attend classes with them. Some school districts have ruled that children with AIDS cannot attend regular classes but must be tutored at home. In Queens, New York, when a second-grader with AIDS was allowed to register for school, angry parents boycotted the school system and kept their children home. Medical authorities assured them that there was no danger. AIDS cannot be spread by casual contact. "How can we be sure?" parents countered. "The disease is still so new, all the evidence isn't in yet." In the town of Washington, New Jersey, people became so panicky that parents pulled their children out of school when the healthy brother of a child with ARC was permitted to attend classes.

There are heated emotions on both sides of the issue, and both viewpoints are understandable. Parents who do not want AIDS children attending school with their children say that we don't know enough yet to be sure that there is no risk. If specialists are wrong, their children might die. Some health workers point out that school has risks for the AIDS children, too. Colds and other infections constantly make the rounds of the school population. AIDS-infected children have lowered immunity, and a virus that might send a healthy child to bed with the sniffles for a day or two could become a life-threatening illness for a child with AIDS. And it isn't as though the children are being deprived of an education, people say, since arrangements are made for home instruction.

That's not good enough, counters the other side. Each child in the United States is guaranteed the right to an education of equal quality, and a couple of hours a day of home tutoring isn't as good as the instruction a child receives in school. In addition, being forced to remain at home, unable to associate with other children on an equal basis, reinforces the AIDS child's feelings of isolation, the sense of being "different" from other children. This can be psychologically damaging.

Some parents and guardians of AIDS children have gone to court to demand the right to send their children to school. One of them is Doris Williams, a Plainfield, New Jersey, nurse who has three small foster children. Two of them are twin girls who were both ready to start kindergarten in the fall of 1985. But one of them has AIDS, acquired as a baby from a contaminated blood transfusion that she received during a serious illness. For several years she suffered from repeated bouts of pneumonia, diarrhea, and high fevers, but treatments with antibiotics and gamma globulin brought all her symptoms under control.

Doris Williams pointed out that the little girl's twin sister, who had slept in the same crib and shared toys with her all her life, showed no signs of AIDS antibodies. Five other children in the family were also perfectly healthy. Schooling at home with a tutor was just not the same, Doris Williams contended. The previous year, when the other children in the family attended a pre-school program from which the AIDS child was banned, "She was the only kid at home, and she felt it. Every time her sister came home from school, she'd say, 'What happened today?' and she'd get all upset." Court battles dragged on, as state officials ordered the child admitted at least to special classes, the local school board took delaying actions, and parent groups continued their protests.

Ryan White, of Kokomo, Indiana, is another child whose life has been turned upside down by AIDS. A friendly, intelligent young teenager who looks like "the boy next door," Ryan is different in two important ways: He suffers from hemophilia; and in 1985, when he complained of feeling tired

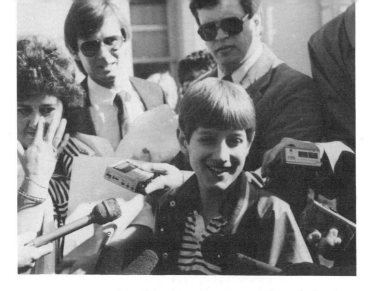

Ryan White, surrounded by friends and reporters, after a judge threw out a temporary injunction barring him from attending classes at Western Middle School near Kokomo. Ryan's mother, Jeanne, is at left.

and ill, doctors discovered that he has AIDS. After missing a term of school, battling AIDS-related infections, Ryan was feeling better and was eager to get back to his friends in the seventh grade. But Kokomo school officials decided that he must stay at home instead, and they set up a telephone linkup with his classroom. Ryan's mother went to court to demand that he be allowed to attend regular classes. Meanwhile, the boy tried to understand what all the fuss was about. He was running a paper route, he said, and going all over the neighborhood, and nobody minded. So how was this so different from going to school? In early 1986, county health officials agreed and ordered the school to readmit Ryan to regular classes. Parent protests sent him home again after only a day, but eventually a court decision put him back in school.

One by one the court cases are settled. In some areas, such as Swansea, Massachusetts, children with AIDS have been accepted by the community and allowed to attend school without any fuss. In the light of growing evidence that AIDS is not transmitted by casual contact, health officials hope this kind of calm sanity in public attitudes will spread and help the youngest AIDS victims cope with their problems instead of adding to them.

6

The World Reacts

In Genoa, Italy, police demand gloves before they will touch a young girl who looks ill and is wandering aimlessly around a public park.

*   *   *

In Hollywood, the Screen Actors Guild takes the position that members can refuse to do scenes involving openmouthed kissing.

*   *   *

Lauren Burk, wife and mother of AIDS victims and herself suffering from ARC, speaks warmly of the support and understanding of people in her Pennsylvania hometown, of the bosses who invited her to come back to work, the friends and relatives who help out with household chores, and the teacher who insisted that her healthy young daughter, Nicole, join a dance class.

*   *   *

In scattered instances, ambulance workers refuse to transport AIDS patients to the hospital, and funeral-parlor employees refuse to handle the bodies of AIDS victims who have died. Firemen in various U.S. communities use a special plastic shield for mouth-to-mouth resuscitation.

*   *   *

A Michigan man, arrested for drunken driving, warns the police officers that he has AIDS and then spits at them. Prosecutors charge him with assault with intent to murder. Acknowledging that spitting can't transmit AIDS, they compare the accused to an assailant armed with a defective gun.

*   *   *

After fifty-six years in business, the AID Insurance Company holds a contest to pick a new name to get rid of "that awful word." Meanwhile, the makers of Ayds appetite suppressant report an increase in sales and say, "Let the disease change its name."

*   *   *

A private testing firm in Los Angeles introduces "tamperproof" I.D. cards certifying that the bearer is free of the AIDS virus antibody. The company touts the cards as a way to stop the spread of AIDS, but the L.A. city council calls for a probe of this new way to "make a buck off another person's misfortune."

*   *   *

A New York physician takes a trip to Mexico and smuggles in a supply of experimental drugs to treat his AIDS patients, then tells his story to a national magazine, risking his license and his liberty to publicize a cause he believes in.

*   *   *

A homosexual AIDS patient in San Francisco returns from the hospital to the apartment he shared with his lover and discovers that the lock on the door has been changed and his clothes and belongings are stacked in cartons on the sidewalk.

*   *   *

In Los Angeles, a volunteer worker for an AIDS support group helps a dying patient make his will and arrange for his funeral, then reaches out to hug him. He cries and tells her, "No one's touched me in so long."

*   *   *

The AIDS epidemic has inspired tales of courage and compassion, along with ironic footnotes to the ongoing human comedy. It has also brought nightmarish scenes that resemble the plagues of the Middle Ages, when the bodies of dead loved ones were thrown into the streets to be carted away and burned in heaps in the village square. Controversies have raged about conflicting rights and inflicted wrongs.

1985 seemed to be the year of AIDS awareness. There was hardly an issue of a newspaper or magazine without an article on AIDS, as parents sued for the right to send their AIDS children to school and other parents loudly protested the violation of their children's rights; as public figures called for quarantines of gays and other members of risk groups, while other public figures warned of the evils of discrimination; as the gaunt, tired faces of AIDS victims appeared on TV talk shows and in print and became as familiar as the faces of movie stars. Then, suddenly, we learned that a real movie star *was* an AIDS victim.

The announcement in August of 1985 that movie-idol Rock Hudson, who had been a romantic symbol for millions, was dying of AIDS did more than any other single event to shock the public into the realization that this disease is a deadly threat that can affect anyone. On October 3, 1985, the day of Hudson's death, the U.S. House of Representatives nearly doubled the funds appropriated for AIDS research, to $189 million, and on the following day the Senate Appropriations Committee raised the total of AIDS funding to $221 million.

Public awareness of the AIDS problem was expanded further as the disease became a popular theme in fictional dramas. Two hit plays, *As Is* and *The Normal Heart,* featured sensitive treatments of the loves and trials of men dying of AIDS. A segment of the *Trapper John* TV series dealt with the dilemmas of a hospital treating an AIDS patient. The disease even found its way into a sitcom: An episode of the Showtime series *Brothers* began with the studio audience laughing at one-liners and ended in stunned silence as characters grappled with questions like "How do you deal with the fact that death comes from loving?" *An Early Frost,* a TV movie about a young lawyer with AIDS, won critical acclaim and stirred intense interest among nearly fifty million viewers all over the U.S. The leading characters of the AIDS dramas were gay men, but the stories were presented as broader human problems affecting everyone.

The growing threat of AIDS has provoked a variety of reactions and is producing major changes in our way of life. When the deadly disease at first seemed to be restricted to homosexuals—especially the promiscuous ones—and drug addicts, many people called the "gay plague" a divine judgment and a punishment for immorality. Then, as the list of AIDS victims grew to include newborn infants and happily married heterosexual couples, such statements seemed increasingly foolish and cruel. Yet homosexual and bisexual men still remain the main AIDS risk group in the United States, and the spread of the disease has brought some backlash against gays. There have been instances of discrimination against gays in housing, jobs, and insurance policies, and morality and gay rights have been made political issues in some local elections. In 1985 Houston mayor Kathy Whitmire was reelected after a bitter campaign in which her opponent criticized her tolerance of the gay life-style and the spread of pornography and made a remark that was inadvertently broadcast live on television: that one way to combat AIDS in Houston would be to "shoot the queers." In New York City, the gay community celebrated the end of a fifteen-year struggle for a homosexual rights bill when the City Council passed the measure in 1986. The bill prohibits discrimination based on sexual orientation in housing, employment, or public accommodation. In other communities, however, old laws against sodomy (oral or anal sexual activity) have been used selectively against gays, with the rationale of stopping the spread of AIDS. Such laws exist in about half the states of the United States but had rarely been enforced.

Discrimination against AIDS patients themselves has now been made illegal in some communities. The Supreme Court has agreed to hear a test case to determine whether people with AIDS and other contagious diseases are protected under

Mayor Ed Koch of New York City, center, signing a homosexual rights bill.

the broader restrictions on discrimination against the handicapped. Communities already have various regulations to protect their members against carriers of contagion. These laws include quarantines that bar people with certain diseases from school, work, and other normal contacts. So far AIDS is not on the list of diseases requiring quarantine, as health officials of Cleveland and Houston discovered when they tried to control the activities of an AIDS victim who was continuing to work as a male prostitute and admitted to engaging in unprotected sexual practices. In 1986 the United States Public Health Service proposed that AIDS be added to the official list of "dangerous contagious diseases." Under Federal law, aliens with such diseases can be prevented from entering the country.

A group of state legislators in Pennsylvania want to go further. They have proposed a state law that would make it a crime for anyone who has AIDS or is carrying the AIDS virus to touch an uninfected person on the genitals, breast, or buttocks, even if the person is clothed. A first offense would be a misdemeanor, but a repeat offense would be a felony. The bill is not considered likely to get out of committee, much less become law.

In June 1986, however, Assistant Attorney General of the United States Charles Cooper added new fuel to the debate, ruling that an employer could legally discriminate against AIDS virus carriers, as long as the hiring or firing decision was based on a fear that the person might spread disease. According to this Justice Department opinion, it makes no difference whether or not there is any real basis for such fears, and AIDS virus carriers are not entitled to protections for the handicapped. Dismayed doctors and public health officials objected that there was no medical or scientific basis for such a ruling. They fear that it will make people reluctant to have their blood tested and will hamper efforts to stop the spread of AIDS.

Legal or not, discrimination against AIDS patients happens all too often. Some hospital workers have refused to care for them, although others have cared with selfless devotion, identifying emotionally with their patients and grieving when they died. AIDS victims have been evicted from their homes and fired from their jobs. Some friends and relatives have been sympathetic and supportive and built a new loving closeness, but others have abandoned the AIDS sufferers and treated them like lepers.

One man tells about returning from the hospital after a bout with pneumonia to find that he had lost not only his job but also his entire support network of friends. "I asked a lady friend, an exercise instructor, to work out a program of exercises for me," he says, "to strengthen the muscles that had gotten weak while I was lying in the hospital."

At first she agreed, but the next day she called him back. "I'm sorry," she said, "but I just couldn't handle it, being in the same room with you."

"This was a woman I'd known for years," he muses unbelievingly. "We were friends. We'd dated . . ." Eventually he moved back to his childhood home and received the love and help he needed from his family and a local AIDS support group.

People who shun AIDS patients and treat them like lepers are acting out of fear and ignorance. Polls have shown that in spite of all the efforts to educate the public on the subject, most people still think you can catch AIDS by sharing a drinking glass, or from a towel or a swimming pool. Panic reactions have sometimes been so severe that a new term has been coined for them: AFRAIDS, standing for "acute fear regarding AIDS."

The AIDS antibody tests that are helping to make our blood supply safe are also raising some disturbing questions. Should a prospective blood donor with a positive antibody test be told? It might seem that the person has the right to know. But since most people infected by the virus probably will not develop the disease, the knowledge could result in years of needless worry. Should blood banks be required to report the identity of donors with positive antibody tests to health authorities as a possible health risk? Some people are fearful that this information might not be kept confidential and might result in various forms of discrimination against the virus-carriers. Such fears are becoming increasingly realistic as the use of AIDS testing spreads. Early in 1986 the Public Health Service proposed that millions of Americans in high-risk groups voluntarily take periodic blood tests to determine whether they have been exposed to the AIDS virus.

Some insurance companies refuse to insure people from the main AIDS risk groups, sometimes asking personal questions of friends and neighbors to determine whether a prospective policyholder is a homosexual or a drug user. Now some of them are using the "AIDS test" to screen out bad insurance risks. The companies do have a legitimate interest in reducing their risks of insuring people who are likely to die or become disabled within a short time, but they are disregarding the fact that current tests do not detect the disease but merely show that a person has been infected with the virus. The group of AIDS virus carriers, overall, are poorer insurance risks than the general population, but nobody yet knows what the real probability is that a particular person with a positive antibody test will develop the disease. Responding to the problem, several states have passed laws barring the use of antibody testing for insurance applicants, and insurance companies are trying to figure out how to predict and cover the costs of AIDS.

America's largest employer, the U.S. Armed Forces, has set up a program to screen both recruits and current personnel for AIDS antibodies. Recruits with a positive test are rejected. Current personnel who test positive are kept in their present jobs, or in whatever jobs they can perform if they develop ARC, and are retired with medical benefits if they come down with AIDS. Military officials justify the program with the argument that they must be able to send personnel anywhere in the world on short notice, without worrying about whether they are weakened by AIDS; and also that military personnel are "walking blood banks" who may be called upon to give blood for a transfusion in an emergency situation. People who object to the testing program argue that it is based on discrimination against homosexuals rather than on medical reasons, and that it will set a dangerous example that may be used by civilian employers to justify discrimination.

There are signs that these fears may have some foundation. A Dallas, Texas, energy firm began requiring food-service employees and applicants for these jobs to be tested for AIDS in 1985, after a worker in the executive dining room was hospitalized with the disease, even though U.S. Public Health Service guidelines state that there is no reason for routine screening of health-care personnel, food handlers, or personal-service workers. In New Jersey, the Bedminster Township Board of Education announced a plan to screen teachers and staff for drug use and AIDS. Such moves have been violently opposed by civil liberties groups. The protests have won considerable support from the public, and the Bedminster school board dropped the plan for a testing program.

Gays demonstrating for the fight against AIDS and against discrimination.

The threat of AIDS has resulted in major changes in life-style, especially in the gay community. The sixties and seventies were the years of the "sexual revolution," when many of the values and moral codes of earlier generations were set aside. Casual sex became more acceptable. Some members of the gay community carried the new "pleasure ethic" to an extreme in bathhouses, where for the modest price of a locker rental a man could engage in sexual activity with as many as fifteen or twenty anonymous partners in an evening. This kind of situation was the perfect breeding ground for a disease like AIDS. In the eighties, as people began to realize that an evening's pleasure might be paid for with a death sentence, the majority of gays began to heed the warnings, limiting the number of their sex partners and avoiding potentially dangerous activities in favor of "safe sex."

Some men have continued to visit the bathhouses, arguing fatalistically that they probably have already been exposed, and, "Either you're going to get it, or you're not." But they are a small minority. Dating has come into fashion among gay couples, and increasing numbers are pairing up into faithful monogamous relationships. Ned Weeks, the hero of the play *The Normal Heart,* complains, "The gay leaders who created this sexual liberation philosophy in the first place have been the death of us. Why didn't they fight for the right to get married instead?"

Although the AIDS epidemic has been producing a great leap backward in our permissiveness toward sexual practices, it has been working to make our society more permissive in terms of what is considered acceptable to talk about in public. The media at first had a cautious attitude toward the reporting of facts on AIDS. They tended to use euphemisms, talking around the touchy subjects instead of reporting them directly.

When both sex and excretory functions are taboo subjects, how can you talk about something like anal intercourse? "Intimate sexual contact" became a popular catchphrase for the main way the AIDS virus is transmitted. Gradually reporters realized that they were unintentionally helping to feed the AIDS panic. Because they weren't saying exactly how people catch AIDS, the public was getting the mistaken impression that almost any kind of activity—even a kiss or a hug—could spread the deadly virus. Now, more and more, the facts are being presented and discussed openly and without embarrassment.

7

Toward the Conquest of AIDS

In the fall of 1985, the United States Public Health Service announced a long-term, three-stage plan for bringing AIDS under control. The plan set specific goals and outlined a timetable for achieving them. The first goal, to be achieved by 1987, is to stem the steady increase in the transmission of the AIDS virus from individual to individual. The second goal, with a target date of 1990, is to reduce the steady increase in the disease itself. The final goal, targeted for the year 2000, is to eliminate the spread of the virus by means of a vaccine to prevent the disease, or effective treatments to cure it. For some years after that goal is achieved, new cases of AIDS will continue to appear among people who have already been infected. But eventually the disease will disappear.

Are these goals realistic? Medical specialists believe the first two can be achieved without any new scientific advances. With tests to screen donor blood, we are already virtually eliminating blood and blood products as a source of new AIDS cases. Changes in behavior can help to reduce the transmission of the virus and the development of AIDS among people in the main risk groups, as well as in the public at large. The changes in behavior that are already taking place in the gay community have been aided by the efforts of federal and local public health agencies, as well as private groups, in publicizing information on safer sexual practices. In Los Angeles, billboards advertise: "L.A. Cares—like a mother. Play safely." Booklets provide detailed advice on "safe sex" techniques, emphasizing the avoidance of activities in which body fluids are transferred. Even in bathhouses, which AIDS physician James Oleske has described as "dens of iniquity," prominent posters give pointers on how to avoid AIDS, and free condoms are provided to the patrons. Because of the long incubation period of AIDS, it is too early to know how much of an effect these changes in behavior are having on the spread of the disease. A general leveling off of the numbers of new AIDS cases in cities with a large gay population has proved in some areas to be only a temporary fluctuation; and a study in New York challenged whether the majority of gays are really following safe sex guidelines—and whether such measures are really effective when close to half the gay population may already be carrying the virus. However, the rates of other sexually transmitted diseases, such as syphilis, gonorrhea, and herpes, are dropping sharply among gay men, and the AIDS statistics may eventually follow the same pattern.

The IV drug abusers are a more difficult group to reach, however. New York City has launched a poster campaign in subways and "shooting galleries" where drug users gather. Posters deliver the message, "AIDS is deadly—don't pass the spike." It is uncertain how many drug addicts are heeding such warnings: According to the city health department, by 1985 AIDS had become the leading cause of death among men aged 30 to 44 and women aged 25 to 29. Fear of AIDS is believed to be causing some addicts to switch to a form of cocaine called "crack," a drug that is smoked rather than injected.

In New Jersey, where the numbers of AIDS cases among drug addicts are much higher than the national averages (IV drug users account for 80 percent of AIDS cases in the city of Newark), a pioneering educational program has been set up to reach this risk group. Former drug addicts have been hired to walk the streets of cities and hang out where drug users gather, spreading the word about the dangers of AIDS and providing practical information to stop the spread of the disease. They warn against sharing "works" (needles and syringes), tell the addicts how to sterilize them by soaking for half an hour in a solution of household bleach, and try to persuade them to join drug-treatment programs. Because these AIDS educators are former addicts themselves, drug users are more willing to listen to them than to health officials, and some users are beginning to change their behavior.

At a conference in Newark in April 1986, a Dutch health official told about a controversial needle exchange program begun in Amsterdam in 1984. Drug addicts can turn in used needles for sterile new ones. The government-sponsored program distributed about 100,000 sterile needles in 1985, with the idea that if the addicts could not be cured, at least the risks of their spreading AIDS could be reduced. A New Jersey Health Department representative suggested that a similar program should be tried in New Jersey, the only state in the United States where the number of IV drug users with AIDS is greater than that of homosexual and bisexual men with the disease.

Effective programs for curbing AIDS in drug users are vital in the fight against AIDS. Drug users can transmit the disease to their sex partners and children, and thus may help to spread AIDS into the general population. The virus can sweep through the drug-using community with frightening speed: Blood tests in Italy indicate that although only 6 percent of drug users tested positive for AIDS antibodies in 1985, by 1986 about 75 percent of the drug users were infected with the virus!

Pointing to the experience in Africa, where AIDS is basically a heterosexual disease, health authorities and medical researchers feared that the disease might soon sweep through the general public in the United States and Europe as well. So far, at least, that predicted epidemic has failed to occur. The proportion of AIDS cases known to be transmitted by sexual activity between men and women has remained at a very low level. Whether the African form of the disease is somewhat different, or is spread among African men and women mainly by nonsexual routes, or whether local customs and the general level of health play the key role in determining how many of those infected actually come down with AIDS—all this is still to be worked out. In Haiti a disturbing shift in the pattern of AIDS cases has already appeared. Although the disease occurred at first mainly in bisexuals, IV drug users, and recipients of transfusions, now these risk groups account for only 11 percent of new AIDS cases, and the proportion of women with AIDS and ARC has risen dramatically. In the United States, screening of military recruits has revealed higher levels of AIDS virus infection than expected, with a much lower ratio of infected men to women than the 13 to 1 currently observed in AIDS patients. Because of the long incubation period of the disease and the large numbers of people believed to be already infected, an epidemic of heterosexual AIDS in the United States may yet appear. Indeed, Public Health Service officials project that unless more effective measures are taken, by 1991 the number of cases among heterosexuals who do not use drugs will have risen to 9 percent of the total, and AIDS will be killing 54,000 people a year—more than the total of auto accident deaths.

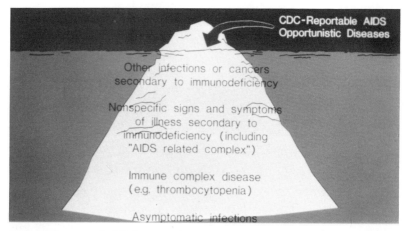

CDC-Reportable AIDS Opportunistic Diseases

Other infections or cancers secondary to immunodeficiency

Nonspecific signs and symptoms of illness secondary to immunodeficiency (including "AIDS related complex")

Immune complex disease (e.g. thrombocytopenia)

Asymptomatic infections

Reported cases of AIDS are only the "tip of the iceberg" of illness that infection with the AIDS virus can cause.

Health authorities fear that the next big rise in AIDS cases may be among young people—teenagers who may become infected when they experiment with sex or drugs. Medical researchers in New York, studying sexual practices of high school students, found that a student's first sexual contact is often with someone about five years older, who has had a greater chance of being exposed to AIDS. The second contact is most often with other teenagers. Considering the substantial percentages of adults who are carrying the virus, especially among sexually active gay males and IV drug abusers in large cities, there is a frightening potential for the spread of AIDS to the younger age groups. Catching AIDS is no longer necessarily associated with promiscuity; a single unprotected intimate contact may be all that is needed for transmission of the virus.

What is needed is effective education as early as the junior high school level. Major cities like New York are setting up educational programs in the public schools to cope with this health threat. The course on AIDS is usually taught as part of the family-living and sex-education curriculum. In colleges the rates of sexually transmitted diseases in general have been greatly reduced by the use of brochures, lectures, films, and counseling through the health services. Hotlines are now also providing AIDS information, and are helping to stop the spread of the disease as well as fear and panic.

In some communities it may be difficult to win acceptance for AIDS education programs. In some areas even the basic facts of sex education are taboo. Parents fear that providing information on the subject would imply approval of promiscuous behavior. Presenting the necessary facts about AIDS involves discussing some aspects of sexual activity that portions of the population consider sinful. Both parents and educators may be uncomfortable with the terms and concepts involved, and yet at this point education is our most powerful weapon for stopping the spread of AIDS and the misunderstandings about the disease.

As for the third goal—eliminating the spread of AIDS with vaccines or treatments—the medical community has an inspiring example to point to. Smallpox used to be a dreaded killer disease. This disease has now been eliminated all over the world. The only smallpox viruses that remain are stored in laboratory cultures for scientific studies. Smallpox was eliminated by a worldwide effort to vaccinate the whole population in all the areas where the disease was a major health problem. Can we do this for AIDS, too? There are some reasons for believing that this would be much more difficult.

The AIDS virus is not a single form but a variety of related viruses. The antigens on the surface of the virus particles differ from one type to another. A vaccine effective against one form of AIDS virus might not work against another. That kind of variation does not occur in the smallpox virus, and the same standard vaccine was used all over the world.

Scientists do have some experience in fighting viruses that occur in varying forms and—like the AIDS virus—mutate or change from one form to another. The flu virus does this, and although we haven't wiped out influenza completely, we have been able to keep up with its changes well enough to produce effective new vaccines when epidemics of new strains break out. Another characteristic of the AIDS virus that may hamper efforts to wipe it out by vaccination is the fact that a very similar disease occurs in green monkeys. These animals may act as a reservoir that could reintroduce AIDS into the human population after it had seemed to be eliminated.

Researchers are making progress toward developing an AIDS vaccine. They have found small numbers of effective antibodies in the blood of AIDS patients, and even larger numbers in the blood of people with ARC. Since vaccines work by stimulating the production of antibodies against the antigens on a germ, this finding means that it should be possible to produce effective vaccines against AIDS. It also suggests some intriguing new lines of research: Are the symptoms of ARC milder because the antibodies are helping to fight the virus, or are people with ARC just producing more antibodies because their illness is not so far advanced? It may be that people who are infected with the virus but do not develop a full-blown case of AIDS have more effective ways of producing antibodies, and if researchers can find out what they are, they may be able to duplicate them.

Another interesting observation is that only a tiny fraction of hemophiliacs exposed to the AIDS virus before procedures were changed to make blood factors safe came down with the disease. Researchers wonder whether something in the process by which blood-clotting factors are concentrated kills or disables the virus and makes it easier for the body to combat it. If so, they can use a variation of the same technique to make a vaccine with killed or weakened AIDS viruses. Other researchers are studying the AIDS-like virus in green monkeys, which do not become ill; they are trying to find out whether the green monkeys' bodies have a special way of handling the virus that might be adapted for humans. Research teams working in Africa have recently reported finding viruses that are related both to the monkey virus and to the human AIDS virus. One form seems very similar to the human virus but does not appear to cause disease. Another does seem to cause AIDS-like symptoms. Studies of these and other naturally occurring viruses may cast some light on what makes the AIDS virus so deadly and may give scientists new knowledge they can use in making a vaccine.

Researchers have been isolating and cloning genes from the AIDS virus, and they hope to use portions of the virus to make vaccines that are safer than live-virus vaccines. They are also finding some virus antigens that different varieties of the virus have in common. Vaccines produced against these antigens might continue to be effective even if the virus mutates. One such antigen may be a protein called gp120, which was synthesized early in 1986. Researchers who injected the natural version of the protein into goats found that they produced antibodies against it. These antibodies protected human cells in culture from infection by AIDS virus. Since the gp120 protein remained unchanged in thousands of generations of the virus growing in T-cell cultures, it is a good prospect for a safe and effective AIDS vaccine.

The gp120 protein is part of the AIDS virus coat. Some researchers believe that an even more effective way to produce a "subunit vaccine" to protect against infection by the whole virus is to base it on a protein from the virus core. The core proteins are much less likely to vary from one virus strain to another. National Cancer Institute researchers have produced an antiserum against thymosin alpha 1, a hormone produced by the thymus gland that is chemically similar to the gag protein from the core of the AIDS virus. In laboratory tests, the antiserum stopped the AIDS virus from infecting human cells, suggesting that effective vaccines could be produced on the basis of core proteins.

In another vaccine approach, genetic engineering techniques have been used to insert DNA copies of AIDS virus genes into vaccinia virus, which has been used for centuries to vaccinate people against smallpox. An injection of the bioengineered vaccinia could stimulate the production of antibodies against AIDS virus, in addition to the smallpox protection. Bioengineered vaccines are already being tested on chimpanzees. Researchers hope to beat the long-range deadline and have AIDS vaccines ready for use on humans years before the end of the century.

Meanwhile, progress is also being made toward finding effective treatments for people who already have AIDS. Some of the experimental drugs that are being tested were described in Chapter 4. Even if they do prove effective, there is an important problem scientists will have to solve to be able to cure AIDS. In addition to attacking T cells, the virus also invades brain cells. It can remain there for years, potentially able to come out and attack the T cells all over again if the body's immune defenses have been restored. But most chemicals—including some drugs being tested against AIDS—normally do not pass from the blood into the brain. To wipe out the virus in an AIDS patient, it will be necessary to work out ways to get the drug past this blood-brain barrier. The combination drug-therapy trials with ribavirin and isoprinosine, for example, include the experimental drug selenazofurin to help ribavirin cross the blood-brain barrier.

Another promising drug that is able to pass into the brain is AZT (azidothymidine). AZT, which is chemically very similar to one of the natural building blocks used to build DNA, prevents the AIDS virus from multiplying. Infected cells, under the direction of virus genes, can add an AZT to the growing DNA chain, but then no further building blocks can be added. The drug has shown encouraging results in trials on AIDS patients and is scheduled for wider testing. Most of the patients who took the experimental drug regained some of the weight they had lost. They had fewer fevers and infections and generally felt better. Tests showed an increase in the number of helper T cells in their blood, along with an improvement of their ability to respond to challenges by foreign antigens. No AIDS virus could be detected in the T cells of the patients who received high doses of AZT. Thus, the drug successfully blocked the virus from multiplying and allowed the immune system to recover somewhat. Since AZT can pass into the brain, it may also be effective against viruses lurking there.

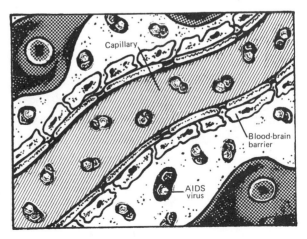

The blood-brain barrier screens the chemicals that are permitted to pass from the blood into the brain cells.

Ethical dilemmas in the testing and use of drugs against AIDS continue to arise. In 1985 a group of French researchers called a press conference to report promising preliminary results with the drug cyclosporine. At the time of the press conference, there were results on only a week of testing, conducted on two patients. Prominent scientists around the world called the French researchers' action irresponsible. The French team defended the decision to go public with their findings at such an early stage with the argument that cyclosporine is a legally available drug that other doctors could begin testing immediately. Their results were so dramatic that it seemed "ethically necessary" to bypass the usual scientific channels and get the news out quickly. In the weeks that followed, reports of the death of one of the original cyclosporine patients and others treated with the drug demonstrated that the French report had indeed been premature. But what kind of timetable is appropriate for testing and reporting on drugs against a disease as deadly as AIDS? That is still in dispute. Meanwhile, the French researchers now claim that cyclosporine, while disappointing in treating full-blown AIDS, may help to restore the immune system in patients with ARC.

Considering the desperation of many AIDS patients, suffering from a disease that is usually fatal and has no proven cures, it is not surprising that many are turning to unconventional approaches. These range from vitamin supplements and special diets to a program involving drinking large amounts of deionized water to rid the body of "toxins." There are also various remedies that treat AIDS as an emotional rather than a viral disease. In the opinion of medical specialists, some of these approaches may be helpful, some neither help nor harm, and some can be downright dangerous. Even treatments that are harmless but ineffective can be dangerous for

AIDS patients if they keep the patients from getting appropriate medical care. Although conventional medicine cannot yet cure AIDS, there are effective treatments for many of the opportunistic infections that kill the victims of this disease.

Among the unconventional treatments, the use of massive doses of vitamin C is claimed to be effective in curing *Pneumocystis carinii* pneumonia, when it is used together with sulfa drugs. In Boston, New York, and Miami, a macrobiotic diet of whole grains, cooked vegetables, beans, soybean products, seaweed, and fish has become a popular alternative for AIDS patients. In one study of twenty-four Kaposi's sarcoma patients, the levels of helper T cells stabilized, and total lymphocyte counts returned to normal after a year on a macrobiotic diet. Six of the patients ultimately died, but the average survival of the group has been more than two years, comparable to that of more conventional treatments.

Doctors emphasize that for progress against AIDS, we need controlled studies, rather than individual patients taking drugs and other treatments on their own. Law enforcement authorities are also concerned about dishonest practitioners who sell worthless treatments to frightened patients for large sums of money.

Some of the most significant advances in the treatment of AIDS may come by following up lines of research that scientists haven't even thought of yet. In a number of laboratories, researchers are conducting basic studies on the nature of the virus and the changes it produces in the body. They have already made interesting findings that may have practical applications.

For example, it has been known for some time that the AIDS virus attacks helper T cells, but recent studies in California have revealed effects on another kind of white blood cells, called granulocytes. These white cells play a key role in the immune defenses: In the normal body, granulocytes detect chemicals from foreign organisms or changed body cells and go after the invaders, gobbling them up and killing them. Researchers do not believe the AIDS virus attacks granulocytes directly, but somehow it makes them less able to move toward invaders and attack them. Whatever is inhibiting the granulocytes is found in the liquid part of the blood: When normal granulocytes are placed in a test tube containing blood serum from AIDS patients, the granulocytes start acting sick. The researchers are trying to identify the chemical that inhibits the granulocytes. If they find a way to counter its effects, they can restore at least part of the AIDS patients' immune defenses.

It has recently been discovered that in addition to attacking white blood cells and brain cells, the AIDS virus also infects a certain type of skin cells called Langerhans cells. These cells are part of the immune system; they pick up antigens and present them to T cells. Langerhans cells are not as easily killed by the AIDS virus as helper T cells. Researchers believe they may act as a reservoir for the virus even after it can no longer be found in an AIDS patient's T cells. Any effective treatment would have to kill the virus hiding in these skin cells, too.

Meanwhile, CDC researchers in Atlanta have discovered how the AIDS virus zeroes in on T-4 lymphocytes (the helper T cells). A protein of the virus, gp110, recognizes and binds to the T-4 protein on the helper T cells. This knowledge could lead to new drugs to block the infection process.

Yale microbiologist Nancy Ruddle reports that infected T cells produce dramatically increased amounts of lymphotoxin, a poison that is part of the normal defenses against tumor cells and germs. Dr. Ruddle suggests that this toxin is what kills the infected T cells and leads to some symptoms of

AIDS, such as weight loss. Finding ways to stop the T cells from producing too much toxin, she suggests, would make AIDS a much less deadly disease that could be treated more effectively with antiviral drugs.

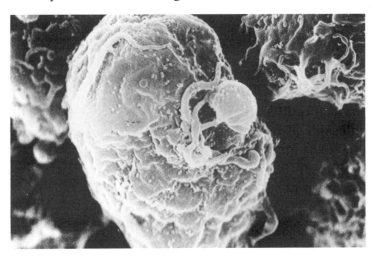

Scanning electron micrograph of an AIDS virus-infected helper T cell. Virus can be seen budding from the cell membrane of the T cell.

A combined effort by research teams from the National Cancer Institute in Bethesda and Harvard University has revealed an AIDS virus gene, tat, that is apparently responsible for the virus's unusually rapid multiplication. The tat gene directs the synthesis of a protein called a transactivator, which stimulates the cell's machinery for making new virus components—including more of the transactivator. The infected cell becomes such an efficient "virus factory" that RNA-directed protein production is increased a thousandfold. This research opens the way to a search for drugs to block the action of the tat gene. In addition, viruses from which the tat gene has been eliminated can be used to produce safe live-virus vaccines, since the altered virus would be unable to reproduce.

The same Harvard team later discovered another AIDS virus gene, art, which unlocks the internal genetic machinery in T cells and permits them to complete the production of new viruses. AIDS viruses with either the art or the tat gene removed could not produce an active infection in cultures of T cells. The art gene is the seventh gene identified in the AIDS virus, which makes it the most complicated of all the retroviruses. This complexity makes the virus deadly, says researcher William Hazeltine, but it is also good news for AIDS fighters because it provides many opportunities to develop drugs against the virus.

An NCI research team, working with Bionetics Research, Inc., has purified reverse transcriptase, the enzyme that the AIDS virus uses to make DNA copies of its RNA, a key stage in its reproduction. The researchers hope to use the purified enzyme for better, faster testing of anti-AIDS drugs. The enzyme was purified with the aid of genetically engineered antibodies. People infected with the AIDS virus generally produce antibodies against reverse transcriptase. These antibodies disappear after symptoms of ARC or AIDS develop. New York researcher Jeffrey Laurence suggests that the antibodies may be a self-defense mechanism protecting infected people against the development of the disease. A long-term study of five thousand healthy gay men, sponsored by the National Institutes of Health, is aimed at determining which antibodies can be used for diagnosing AIDS infection and whether any particular antibodies are indications of T-cell protection.

American, French, and Israeli researchers have found that antigens that stimulate the immune system have a dramatic effect on AIDS virus-infected T cells, causing them to release the AIDS virus and die. These laboratory studies explain how promiscuous sexual behavior, which may expose people to

blood, semen, or germs (all of which contain foreign antigens), can increase the risk of developing AIDS. They also fit
in with studies such as the joint effort between researchers in
France and the United States that has discovered fragments of
the genes of hepatitis-B viruses inside the blood cells of AIDS
patients. This finding supports the idea that infection with
other viruses may make people more susceptible to AIDS.
Perhaps vaccines against these other viruses will make people
better able to fight off the AIDS virus.

The growth of T cells is controlled by a substance called
T-cell growth factor (interleukin-2), which stimulates the
cells, and by tiny chemical receptors on the surface of the T
cells that detect the presence of the growth factor. National
Cancer Institute researchers, working with a team at Im-
munex, a genetic-engineering company in Seattle, have isolated the gene that produces the T-cell receptors for the
growth factor; a Japanese group is doing similar work. Although practical applications are years away, the gene might
be used to produce large quantities of the receptors. They
could then be given to AIDS patients to turn on the growth of
their T cells. This would be an alternative approach to the use
of interleukin-2, which is showing some promise in treating
AIDS and cancer patients.

Studies like these are going on in laboratories all over the
world. As researchers learn more about AIDS and the virus
that causes it, they are coming closer to achieving their long-
range goal: to eliminate the spread of AIDS and end its
deadly threat to humanity.

Meanwhile, we already have the means to achieve the
short-term goals and limit the ravages of AIDS. We need to
focus on the practical matters of education and prevention.
As June Osborn, dean of the University of Michigan School
of Public Health, points out, we should not allow false hopes

for a quick cure to prevent us from examining our present options and the consequences of our actions. "Prevention," she notes, "is the most rational thing, and is possible—not easy, but possible." Education about the nature of AIDS and the ways to prevent it will help to stop the spread not only of AIDS but also of feelings of fear, blame, and resentment towards AIDS patients and members of the major risk groups. AIDS is not an "us" versus "them" situation. It involves all of us.

Suggested Reading

Robin Marantz Henig, "AIDS: A New Disease's Deadly Odyssey," *New York Times Magazine*, February 6, 1983, pp. 28-44.

Peter Carlson et al., "AIDS: Fatal, Incurable and Spreading," *People*, June 17, 1985, pp. 42-49.

"The New Victims," *Life*, July 1985, pp. 12-19.

Facts About AIDS (pamphlet), U.S. Department of Health and Human Services, Public Health Service, August 1985.

David Gelman et al., "AIDS," *Newsweek*, August 12, 1985, pp. 20-29.

Claudia Wallis et al., "AIDS: A Growing Threat," *Time*, August 12, 1985 pp. 40-47.

Janice Hopkins Tanne, "The Last Word on Avoiding AIDS," *New York*, October 7, 1985, pp. 28-34.

John Langone, "AIDS: Special Report," *Discover*, December 1985, pp. 28-53.

"The Mystery of AIDS," *Science Digest*, January 1986, pp. 40-41, 85.

Joseph Carey, "The Rivalry to Defeat AIDS," *U.S. News and World Report*, January 13, 1986, pp. 67-68.

Morton Hunt, "Teaming Up Against AIDS," *New York Times Magazine*, March 2, 1986, pp. 42-44 and following.

Peter Goldman and Lucille Beachy, "One Against the Plague," *Newsweek*, July 21, 1986, pp. 38-50.

Terms

anal intercourse—sexual activity in which the penis of one partner is inserted into the rectum of the other.

antigen—a chemical (usually a protein or complex carbohydrate) that stimulates the body's immune defenses.

antibody—a protein produced by B cells that can react chemically with a specific antigen.

condom—a protective sheath worn over the penis during sexual activity.

gay—a popular synonym for homosexual (usually male).

heterosexual—a person sexually attracted to members of the opposite sex.

homosexual—a person sexually attracted to members of the same sex.

immune system—B cells and T cells that distinguish between "self" and foreign chemicals and defend the body from invading microbes and cancer.

incubation period—the time between exposure to a germ and the appearance of symptoms of the disease it causes.

IV drugs—drugs such as heroin, taken by injection into a vein.

lesbian—a synonym for a homosexual female.

lymphocytes—white blood cells that function in the immune system; they include B cells and T cells.

opportunistic infection—an illness caused by a bacterium, virus, or parasite that produces symptoms only in people whose immune defenses are already weakened.

oral sex—sexual activity involving contact between the mouth of one partner and the genital organs of the other.

poppers—inhalant drugs used to enhance the pleasurable sensations of sexual activity.

promiscuous—having numerous sex partners.

retrovirus—a virus that contains RNA, which is used as a pattern for the cell to manufacture DNA (genes), which then directs the production of virus components.

reverse transcriptase—an enzyme used by retroviruses to produce DNA.

safe sex—sexual practices designed to minimize the risk of transmitting AIDS, mainly by the use of condoms and other techniques to avoid transferring semen or other body fluids between partners.

semen—fluid released from the penis during sexual activity, containing sperm.

sperm—the male reproductive cells.

vaginal intercourse—sexual activity in which the penis of the male partner is inserted into the vagina of the female partner.

Index